THE CHURCH'S
MINISTRY OF HEALING

THE CHURCH'S
MINISTRY OF HEALING

* * *

A. H. PURCELL FOX
A.K.C.

WITH A FOREWORD BY
THE DEAN OF EXETER

LONGMANS

LONGMANS, GREEN AND CO LTD
6 & 7 CLIFFORD STREET, LONDON W1

THIBAULT HOUSE, THIBAULT SQUARE, CAPE TOWN
605–611 LONSDALE STREET, MELBOURNE C1
443 LOCKHART ROAD, HONG KONG
ACCRA, AUCKLAND, IBADAN
KINGSTON (JAMAICA), KUALA LUMPUR
LAHORE, NAIROBI, SALISBURY (RHODESIA)

LONGMANS, GREEN AND CO INC
119 WEST 40TH STREET, NEW YORK 18

LONGMANS, GREEN AND CO
20 CRANFIELD ROAD, TORONTO 16

ORIENT LONGMANS PRIVATE LTD
CALCUTTA, BOMBAY, MADRAS
DELHI, HYDERABAD, DACCA

First Published 1959

Printed in Great Britain by
The Camelot Press Ltd., London and Southampton

CONTENTS

Part IV

FOREWORD

At a time when so much interest is being expressed in the revival of the Church's Ministry to the Sick this is a very appropriate and opportune little book. The author, the Rev. A. H. Purcell Fox, sometime Assistant Chaplain at the London Hospital and later Chaplain of the Brompton Hospital, Assistant Chaplain of the Guild of St. Raphael, and a parish priest, writes with the authority of a long and varied experience in this ministry, reinforced by wide reading and a very sound capital of common sense. There is nothing sensational in these pages: the author makes no extravagant claims: on the contrary the contents are marked, as one would expect from a leading representative of the Guild, by a commendable restraint free from all theological jargon, so that the book can be easily read even by those who have no previous acquaintance with the subject. It is a book which will be of very great help not only to clergymen but to all men and women who are interested in the whole ministry of the Church, and particularly to those whose minds are confused by the many exaggerated and discordant claims of 'healers' from outside the disciplines of the Church.

ALEXANDER WALLACE

The Deanery,
Exeter

ACKNOWLEDGEMENTS

To the Very Rev. Alexander Wallace, Dean of Exeter, who read the manuscript and kindly wrote the Foreword, and to the Rev. A. W. Hopkinson and the Rev. Henry Cooper who have also afforded me valuable help with comments and criticisms, my sincerest thanks are due.

In no less measure am I indebted to the many members of the medical profession with whom I have been associated in the past and to the patients to whom we have ministered together. In such happy partnerships much experience has been gained which has made this essay possible.

A. H. P. F.

INTRODUCTION

MUCH has been and is being written about Spiritual Healing and many people are confused by the various views and methods of which the writers are the exponents. There are Spiritist 'healers', free-lance 'healers' who claim no allegiance to any particular religious body, healers who employ psychological techniques tinged with a religious colouring, some who have no place to give to the work of medical science, and others who somewhat grudgingly recognise it.

It might seem that enough has already been written. The confusion caused by this spate of literature is serious, especially when it leads the ordinary Churchman to seek in doubtful quarters what he should be able to find in his own Church. He is liable to turn, when in need, to any source of help which first offers itself, and ignorance of what is available in the Church of which he is a member leaves him open to disappointment and danger.

This, then, is an attempt to expound simply for the layman the Church's Ministry to the Sick which embraces her ministry of healing—and more. The Church of England is in no way behind the times, as some people think, in the revival of the healing ministry. On the contrary, she has long ago taken the lead in its restoration and is steadily educating her ministers and people along lines which may be less spectacular and exciting but which are the ways of catholic practice from the earliest times.

We hear from various sources of wonderful 'cures' at the hands of 'healers'. Results which are claimed as marvellous and even miraculous are proclaimed in the popular press, but the failures and relapses are apt to be passed over in silence. In this there are great dangers. Although the Church of England could produce an impressive list of 'successes', she wisely avoids publicity. Her teaching and practice are based on sound theology, but she knows she will not serve the cause of truth and religion by making extravagant claims. She is not concerned to establish a reputation for producing miracles and marvels, but to serve the sick in the name of Christ. Jesus said, "Tell no man" but He also said, "Go and shew thyself to the priest": it is not always easy to decide when we should be reticent and when we should bear witness, but the dangers associated with modern publicity methods must always require of us caution in our utterances and writings about results.

The Church's Ministry to the Sick is a continuation of catholic practice on the tried and traditional lines which have been in use in the Church since Apostolic times. Nevertheless, she takes cognisance of modern developments in medical science and unhesitatingly accepts the work of the medical profession as a gift of God for the healing of His people. The Church, therefore, seeks closer co-operation between priest and doctor as the surest way at the present time of bringing the fullest benefits to the sick. In her ministry to the mentally disordered, for example, the clergy receive the enlightenment brought to them by psychological medicine gladly and gratefully. But the Church's ministry is essentially spiritual, and she seeks to lead men and women to God as the true source of all healing. This she does by the well tried ways of the ministry of the Word, Prayer, and the Sacraments, and is thus "like unto a man that is an householder, which bringeth forth out of his treasure things new and old" (Mt. 13:52).

Conditions change, and the Church must adapt herself to modern circumstances and profit by new knowledge, even when in the interests of truth she must needs be slow to accept every new and untried theory. But through all the changes in man's environment human nature remains basically the same, and the Church's faith is always adequate to the demands made upon it. Man needs redemption, and Christ working in and through His Church brings it to all who know their need and will seek His aid.

The Ministry to the Sick is more extensive than the ministry of healing, if healing is to be regarded as synonymous with the cure of physical and mental ailments. In that sense many, for reasons which cannot always be clear to us, remain uncured. To them the Church must bring the power to endure and to profit from their condition. Death ultimately overtakes us all, and through faith in Christ we must so learn to live that we may meet death as a Christian should.

Moreover, we must not allow the healing ministry to be lifted out of its setting in the larger ministry of the Church, for to do so would be to let it degenerate into a cult. It is but one aspect of God's redemptive power and, although it has been neglected and therefore needs to be brought back to its rightful place, it cannot be made into a sole end in itself without grievous distortion of the whole content of the Christian faith.

There is emphasis on healing because it is impossible to believe that it is God's will that man should be defeated by disease, and because Our Lord's attitude towards sickness plainly shows that healing is a part of the redemptive action of God. In this respect there has been a general reorientation of Christian thought in recent years. This has not introduced a new doctrine, but has revived a truth long neglected. For a long time the priest's ministry to the sick has been received with suspicion, and he himself has often been regarded as the harbinger of death. He still has a ministry to those who are approaching the end of their earthly life, and he must aid and sustain all who are enduring long suffering, but it is, happily, becoming understood that he has also a ministry through which many may find healing as did those to whom Our Lord and His Apostles ministered. He is not the helpless spectator of the march of disease; he can be the bearer of spiritual aids which go far to overthrow it.

One is conscious that many questions will be raised in these pages which cannot be adequately dealt with in a small book and which do not come within its scope. The deeper theological issues can only be given full consideration in a volume which needs to be written on the theological background to the ministry of healing. But it is the hope of the present writer that some who read these pages may be led to look to the Church for the help which is available to them, and also that members of the Anglican Communion may find in them some guidance in the share they can have in bringing the ministry of the Church to the afflicted sons and daughters of our heavenly Father.

PART ONE

1

CHRIST THE HEALER

I came that they may have life, and may have it
abundantly.

JN. 10:10.

WHEN God created man He made him in His own
likeness, not in a physical sense but in a spiritual
sense. He did for him what He had done for no
other creature: "The Lord God formed man of the dust of
the ground, and breathed into his nostrils the breath of life;
and man became a living soul" (Gen. 2:7). However later
generations have interpreted this act of God's creation, it
still remains true that man is the crown of God's work, and
that in moral and spiritual stature he stands unique and far
above all other created things. His body is described as the
"temple of the Holy Ghost" (1 Cor. 6:19), he can know and have
communion with his Maker, he is made "a little lower than
the angels" and is crowned "with glory and honour" (Heb.
2:7). But from this high estate he is fallen, so that, although
he is capable of Godlike greatness, through sin he can sink
to the level of the beast. So we have on the one hand the
saints who have set before us the possibilities of man's spiritual
magnificence, and we have at the other extreme the tragic
examples of his debasement, and "all have sinned and come
short of the glory of God" (Rom. 3:23). It is this sin-weakened
nature which we all inherit at birth, and by ourselves we

cannot change our condition. Its entail of suffering in body, mind and spirit is incalculable, but it is manifestly not what God intended to be man's lot.

The Christian belief is that it is possible for every human soul to be redeemed from this condition, not merely by education or the betterment of his social environment, but by the grace of God, for God has not abandoned us to our lot, but has put out His saving hand. Such is His love for those whom He has made in His own likeness that "God commendeth his love toward us, in that, while we were yet sinners, Christ died for us" (Rom. 5:8), and the Christian Gospel or Good News to mankind is "God so loved the world, that he gave his only begotten Son, that whosoever believeth in him should not perish, but have everlasting life" (Jn. 3:16).

This great act of the Divine Love came to pass when Jesus was born in Bethlehem; when, as St. Paul puts it, "the fulness of the time was come, God sent forth his Son, made of a woman" (Gal. 4:4). It was an event anticipated by the Jewish prophets in that long period which culminated in "the fulness of the time", and Jesus and His Apostles were wont to refer to the witness which the prophets had given of His coming.

In the fourth chapter of St. Luke's Gospel we are told that one Sabbath day Jesus went into the synagogue in Nazareth and read from one of these prophecies the following passage: "The Spirit of the Lord is upon me because . . . he hath sent me to heal the brokenhearted, to preach deliverance to the captives, and recovering of sight to the blind, to set at liberty them that are bruised, to preach the acceptable year of the Lord."[1] Then having closed the book He addressed the congregation and said, "This day is this scripture fulfilled in your ears." (Luke 4:18-19 and 21.)

[1] Is. 61:1.

On another occasion John the Baptist sent two messengers from his prison to ask Jesus, "Art thou he that should come, or do we look for another?" The answer given to them to take back to John was: "Go and shew John again those things which ye do hear and see: the blind receive their sight, and the lame walk, the lepers are cleansed, and the deaf hear, the dead are raised up, and the poor have the gospel preached to them" (Mt. 11:2-5).

Now this was evidence enough that He was the expected Messiah, for the prophets had led the Jews to look forward to one who would bring healing to men, healing both of soul and body. The work of redemption had begun and it was to embrace the whole of man's being. The works of Jesus were to testify that He was sent by God, for He said, "My meat is to do the will of him that sent me, and to finish his work" (Jn. 4:34) and again, "I have greater witness than that of John: for the works which the Father hath given me to finish, the same works that I do, bear witness of me, that the Father hath sent me" (Jn. 5:36).

St. John the Evangelist wrote his Gospel when he was old and had had time for much reflection, and it is significant that he is constantly pointing to the works of Jesus as evidence of the oneness of Christ with God the Father. This is made very clear in the discourse of Jesus with Philip: "Believest thou not that I am in the Father, and the Father in me? the words that I speak unto you I speak not of myself: but the Father that dwelleth in me, he doeth the works. Believe me that I am in the Father, and the Father in me: or else believe me for the very works' sake" (Jn. 14:10-11).

Many people are still thinking that disease is a visitation of a God whose displeasure they have knowingly or unknowingly incurred, and they will misquote Hebrews 12:6: "For whom the Lord loveth he chasteneth, and scourgeth every son whom he receiveth." The writer is quoting from the

Book of Proverbs, and if this passage is read in its context, it will be seen that it has no reference to disease. The experience of sickness may well have a chastening effect upon us, but the healing works of Jesus are the strongest evidence that God seeks to heal men, and not to afflict them with destructive plagues. The impression of a God who strikes men down with disease, culled from some passages of the Old Testament, belongs to an immature concept of God which is completely dispelled in the fuller revelation given to us through Christ and His works. Jesus even "desecrated" the Sabbath by performing healing acts and brought upon Himself severe criticism by doing so, but He contended that there could be no more fitting occupation on the day that is kept holy to God.

The amount of time Christ gave to healing works and the space given to recording them by the Evangelists show us how vital they were to a right concept of God's attitude towards afflicted mankind. Moreover, Jesus was not content Himself to heal, but also specifically commanded His disciples to accompany their preaching of the gospel of the Kingdom with the healing of the sick. When sending out the twelve, He bade them, "As ye go, preach, saying, The kingdom of heaven is at hand. Heal the sick, cleanse the lepers, raise the dead, cast out devils: freely ye have received, freely give" (Mt. 10:7-8), and to the seventy He said, "Heal the sick . . . and say unto them, The kingdom of God is come nigh unto you" (Lk. 10:9). These passages read like the briefing for a great offensive, as indeed they were. The reign of a God of love was to be proclaimed by His acts of love of which healing works were to be some of the visible manifestations.

This commission was not intended to be temporary, for it was repeated, and we may say extended, shortly before our Lord's Ascension. "These signs shall follow them that believe," He is recorded as saying, "In my name shall they cast out devils; they shall speak with new tongues; they shall take up serpents; and if they drink any deadly thing, it shall not hurt them; they shall lay hands on the sick, and they shall recover" (Mk. 16:17-18).[1] If we follow the disciples and apostles in their activities after Our Lord's visible presence had been taken from them, we shall find ample evidence of the statement that "they went forth, and preached everywhere, the Lord working with them, and confirming the word with signs following" (Mk. 16:20).

Christian Science describes Jesus as "the Way-shower", but He declares Himself to be "the way, the truth, and the life" (Jn. 14:6), and the catholic faith is that He is more than a human teacher who propounds truths; He is the Divine Son of God by whose Cross and Passion men are redeemed. It is not by a mere intellectual apprehension of moral and spiritual truths that men can be saved, but by the grace which Christ imparts to those who would follow Him, for without grace we are powerless to overcome what St. Paul calls "the law of sin which is in my members" (Rom. 7:23).

In these days when many esoteric cults are offering "healing" to the public it becomes more than ever necessary to remind Churchpeople that those who would have healing such as Our Lord offered to men must come to Him. In the words of advertisers they should "beware of substitutes", for as Peter was called upon to answer the question "By what power, or by what name, have ye done this?", the reply was, "By the name of Jesus Christ of Nazareth . . . for there is none other name under heaven given among men, whereby we must be saved" (Acts 4:7-12). Any claim to heal

[1] The authenticity of this passage has been questioned and it does not appear in some of the ancient manuscripts, but it has, nevertheless, been included in the Canon of Scripture and, it may be assumed, represents an utterance of Jesus which was subsequently proved in the experience of the Church.

by "religious" methods which are not in the name and spirit of Jesus are not Christian, and although "cures" may be effected, they will be inferior to the healing Our Lord came to bring.

It needs to be emphasised that the healing ministry of the Church is not some system of "new thought" nor a new application of the principles of psychotherapy, but the reconciliation of man to God through the saving power of Jesus Who is the same yesterday, to-day, and for ever. The Church brings sufferers to the Lord of Life through the preaching of the Word, through forgiveness, through prayer and sacrament, and by these ways appointed by the Saviour Himself He stretches out His hand to save and to heal. The redemption He offers is more than the cure of a physical sickness: it is the restoration of our fallen nature to that likeness to God which is our true heritage, and it encompasses the whole of our being, body, mind and spirit.

2

THE CHURCH

He is the head of the Body, the Church.
COL. 1:18.

THE title of this book is "The Church's Ministry of Healing". Some people may think that we talk a lot about the Church and not enough about Christ, as if, somehow, Christ and His Church were two different things. But this is due to a misunderstanding of what we mean by the Church. We often speak of the Church as the Mystical Body of Christ. That is to say that, as Jesus in the days of His bodily presence on earth did and said certain things, now He acts and speaks through that body, the Church, which He formed and to which He committed His work and teaching before He ascended into heaven. The Church is not simply a congregation of human beings, it is not even an organisation for the propagation of Christ's Gospel. It is an *organism*, and an organism is a living thing in and through which life expresses itself. The life which lives within and expresses itself through the Church is the Life of God in Christ. This life courses through the Fellowship as it is in the closest communion with Jesus. So we think of the Church under the simile of the vine, as Jesus Himself said, "I am the vine, ye are the branches. He that abideth in me, and I in him, the same bringeth forth much fruit: for without me ye can do nothing" (Jn. 15:5).

In the church in which I served my first curacy there is a beautiful East window. It depicts the Risen and Ascended

Christ superimposed upon a vine. The branches extend through all the lights of the window encircling the great saints and teachers of the Church and heraldic crests of the Province of Canterbury and of the diocese. The truth which this window proclaims—that all the life of the Church is derived from Him Who is her root, Jesus—is a truth which we must grasp if we are ever to understand the authority of the Church, the efficacy of the sacraments, and the purpose of her other activities. So we know that the Church is a human institution in respect of the humanity of her members, but we know also that she is much more than human. She is divine because Her Lord is divine and apart from His Life which pulses through every part of her she would have no Life at all.

Often the Church is accused of looking back too much to the past. Of course, she must ever be looking forward—she must, as we say, "progress with the times". But progress and adaptation of her purpose to modern needs and conditions do not mean a break with the past. The reason why she is constantly referring back is because, as St. Paul wrote, "Other foundation can no man lay than that is laid, which is Jesus Christ" (1 Cor. 3:11). It has always been a cardinal principle in the Church of England to impose upon none of her members as a matter to be held as "of the faith" any doctrine which cannot be proved or substantiated by reference to the Apostles' teaching as they received it from Our Lord Himself. Departure from this principle leads us into error, either by contradiction, or by producing something new which is not consistent with the "faith which was once de-livered unto the saints" for which St. Jude (verse 3) bids us "earnestly contend". English people have a distrust of what they call "new-fangled notions", but it is surprising how easily they fall victims to strange doctrines in the guise of a religion. This is something we must keep steadily in mind in connection with our subject, for there are many cults and individuals teaching "strange doctrines" about it.

The Church of England, indeed the whole Anglican Communion of which she is but a small part, claims to be a branch of the Catholic Church built, as the Collect for the feast of St. Simon and St. Jude expresses it, "upon the foundation of the Apostles and Prophets, Jesus Christ Himself being the head corner-stone". A faith which is universal or catholic must be "for all men, everywhere, and at all times". This claim to catholicity rests upon the continuity of the Church with its Divine Head and the Apostles whom He commissioned and sent forth in His Name—"As my Father hath sent me, even so send I you" (Jn. 20:21). Her ministry is not a new man-made invention. It is derived from the Apostles and has continued through the ages to the present day, so that what was commanded by Our Lord to the Apostles is still the duty of the bishops and priests who have succeeded them. That which they do in His Name is done with His authority.

But the greater part of the Church consists in its lay members to whom this special ministerial authority has not been given. This does not mean that they have no ministry to perform, nor that they play a merely passive part in the Church's life. On the contrary, as we shall see, they have a large and active share in the Church's ministry to the whole body and to the world at large.

A phrase which Our Lord used, "the Kingdom of God", will appear presently. It means that sphere in which the sovereignty of God is acknowledged and established. This sphere is partially realised in the Church, but it is part of the Church's mission to extend that Kingdom to all mankind. Thus the Church must be missionary to all the world, for the Kingdom which is in existence has yet to be built. It is like an unfinished edifice of which the glory is only known to the

Architect, and dimly seen by its builders. Moreover it is only visible in part, for it extends to the Church invisible, to include those who have gone before us in the faith, to the Church triumphant in the heavens, as well as to millions as yet unborn. Perhaps the relevance of this phrase is most clearly realised when we remember the words of Our Blessed Lord, "I seek not mine own will, but the will of the Father which hath sent me" (Jn. 5:30). These are words which must be appropriated by every member of the Church, for in them lies the key to the building of the Kingdom. It will be necessary to remember them when we have to consider problems concerning God's will in sickness.

The Church, then, is the organ of God's redemptive work in the world. It is God's will that all men should be saved, saved, that is to say, from the results of man's fall which produce so much, perhaps all, of man's misery and ills. Every evil that afflicts mankind is to be overcome, whether it be an individual who suffers or whole communities, but this can only be if we are appropriating to ourselves Christ's redemptive sacrifice and uniting ourselves with Him in fulfilling God's will and purpose. This is to seize hold on life; apart from it there can only be the ultimate triumph of all that is destructive of man's life.

Everyone comes into this world by the process of natural birth. So we share with all created things a body subject to decay and disintegration. It is the Christian faith that even this body shall be "raised a glorious body", and that it is the temple of the Holy Ghost. It is the instrument of the spiritual man, through which God seeks to express Himself in every individual life. In Holy Baptism we are engrafted into that Vine through which the life of God flows; we are raised from the natural to the supernatural. In the life of the Church we inherit all that belongs to the sons of God, health— wholeness of both physical and spiritual life. We can interrupt and fall away from this source of true life by sin, but God in His mercy is able and willing to restore us. Regularly we are spiritually and physically fed with Life in the Holy Communion. Finally we pass from death unto Life as we shed this body of our mortality. All this hope is preserved for us in our life in Christ in the Church. We are like plants constantly fed and watered, as in the sacraments and through prayer we receive grace from God.

So, as we meditate upon the meaning of the Church, we see in it the means by which God works His perfect will for the saving of men and women whom He has created in His own image, and we see this salvation not only as a future hope but as a present reality for all who live in Him. It is a reality vividly brought home to us not only in words but in the healing works of Jesus and His Apostles, and moreover in that healing ministry which continues in the Church to-day.

3

THE REVIVAL OF THE HEALING MINISTRY

He sent them to preach the kingdom of God and to heal the sick.

LK. 9:2.

THE Church has received from Our Lord a commission to exercise a healing ministry. "Heal the sick that are therein," said Jesus to the disciples as He sent them out on their mission to the villages and towns, "and say unto them, The kingdom of God is come nigh unto you" (Lk. 10:9). This was later reinforced by the promise, "Greater works than these shall he do; because I go unto my Father" (Jn. 14:12). The Apostles are seen fulfilling this command and the word is confirmed "with signs following". In the power of the Holy Spirit received at Pentecost the infant Church is able to manifest the healing works which Jesus had promised.

For a long time the Church was the most active agent in the healing of the sick, and soon "guest-houses" were established in which the sick and aged were attended with skill and devotion. Priests and bishops were physicians, and nursing was carried out by women who were sometimes formed into religious orders for the purpose. The modern missionary hospital is the nearest parallel to this in the Church of to-day.

The decline in the healing ministry was coincident with the general failing of faith and Pentecostal zeal which became a marked feature of the period after the issue of the Edict of Constantine. When, after a long epoch of persecution, Christianity became a safe and fashionable religion, it was inevitable that much of its first fire should gradually subside, and it is noticeable that healing power tended to diminish in all periods when faith burned dim.

But many other factors have also contributed to the decline. As time went on, medical science became more and more specialised—skill and knowledge advanced, and practical requirements gradually led to separation from its earlier religious setting and connections. By the nineteenth century the divorce was all but complete, and the rationalistic thought of the times produced a philosophy which left no room for miracles or divine action outside the laws understood by man. Man came to rely more and more upon his own knowledge, and to become more and more the centre of his own universe. Humanism took the place of religious philan-thropy, and has been found in these later days to be inadequate. Nevertheless, the great arts of medicine and surgery have so advanced that we must regard them as some of the wonderful means by which God works to heal and alleviate many human ills. This is no matter for regret, and to-day we are witnessing the great skills of the medical profession being slowly but steadily re-wedded to the contribution which religion has to make to the full healing of mankind; for religion still has a great part to play in healing, and the co-operation of doctor and priest will undoubtedly lead to a new age in the treatment of sickness. We cannot, of course, revert to the conditions of the Apostolic age, but the Church's commission will be fulfilled in ways suited to the modern situation.

Certain events can be seen to be leading to the present revival:

(a) The challenge presented by Christian Science and other cults which have attempted to make up for the neglect of the healing ministry by the Church.

(b) The growth of psychological medicine with its revelation of the wonderful relationship between mind and body.

(c) The re-awakening of large sections of the Christian world to the plain implications of the teaching of Our Lord in the Gospel.

The breakdown of the unity of the Church has been one of the greatest causes of her weakness, and the present movement towards the reunion of Christendom is seen to coincide with a renewed vision of her mission to mankind. As the Church grows stronger in corporate faith and witness, we may expect a progressive revival of those manifestations of Pentecostal power which were characteristic of the great age of faith. Among these will be the powers of healing.

The Church of England is giving a wonderful lead to Christendom in the cause of reunion, and has also taken the lead in the revival of the healing ministry. From time to time statements are made which imply that the Church of England is doing little about Spiritual Healing. The truth, however, is quite the contrary. Spiritual Healing has not only engaged the attention of Lambeth Conferences and committees appointed by them or by Convocation periodically over many years, but it is mainly due to the initiative of the Church that the present widespread interest has been aroused. Even the Roman Catholic communion appears to have been influenced by this. At a Conference held at Vanves in France in 1948 the healing ministry of that branch of the Catholic Church was carefully considered, and some of the recommendations made there were clearly in line with the work done on the subject by the Church of England.[1]

The Guild of St. Raphael which is exclusively Anglican has taken a leading part in the revival for many years. Its aim is, and always has been, to restore to the normal pastoral

---

[1] See 'The Unction of the Sick in the Western Church', by Dr. T. W. Crafer, in *Theology*, September 1949, Vol. LII, No. 351.

ministry of every parish the healing of the sick through the Word and Sacraments. The Guild of Health, which includes members of other churches, is also doing great work. The Divine Healer Mission is mainly but not exclusively Anglican, and has long been doing quiet and valuable work.

The late Archbishop William Temple considered the revival of healing of such importance that he formed a committee to study the subject. This committee became the Churches' Council of Healing which is a consultative and co-ordinating body formed of representatives of the Church of England and many of the Free Church bodies. The President is the present Archbishop of Canterbury.

One of the results of all this work during the past forty years or more has been the authorisation by Convocation of forms for the Laying on of Hands and the Anointing of the Sick. Another has been the winning of the interest of a large section of the medical profession and a Statement[1] from the British Medical Association calling for closer co-operation between doctors and ministers of religion. In several parts of the country groups of doctors and clergy meet to study problems of mutual interest in the treatment of the sick and to seek ways of putting into practice the suggestion made in the Statement. Not least among the results has been the rapid and widespread interest created at home and overseas among both clergy and laity. But the most important result of the work of these years has been the change in the character of the healing ministry in a large and steadily increasing number of parishes.

Nevertheless, there are dangers in all revivals. Extravagances are liable to arise, and even exploitation by charlatans and ill-instructed persons. There are great risks attendant upon certain forms of public healing services and missions,

[1] Published in the Supplement of the *British Medical Journal*, 8 November 1947.

and there are "healers" whose teaching and methods cannot be commended nor recognised by the Church. One of the best safeguards against these dangers is to form a branch or group of such a guild as the Guild of St. Raphael by means of which sound doctrine can be learned and the Church's traditional methods can be introduced and practised in the parish with the certainty that what is taught and done is in accordance with the authority of the Church.

The Archbishops' Commission on Divine Healing, composed of a panel of theologians and doctors, issued a report in 1958 containing much valuable information and guidance based on a very full investigation of the whole matter from the medical and pastoral, as well as the theological, aspect.

Note on the Terms 'Faith Healing', 'Divine Healing', and 'Spiritual Healing'

FAITH HEALING. This term was in frequent use in the earlier stages of the revival of the healing ministry, and is still used by a few people, especially new inquirers. It does not describe the healing ministry satisfactorily because it tends to imply that healing is the result of a concentration of thought by the sufferer on the probability of a cure. Although faith has its proper place in Christian healing it is of a different kind from this. Because of the implication that the onus lies on the patient to produce a desired effect, it is rather in the order of auto-suggestion than of Christian faith. It is, therefore, misleading and for this reason is not generally used.

DIVINE HEALING. Some objection has been raised to this term as suggesting that only healing by means of religious ministrations is of divine origin. Since all healing must come from God who works through medicine and surgery as well as through prayer and sacraments, the term Divine Healing needs to be understood in this wider sense.

SPIRITUAL HEALING. This term is frequently confused with

Spirit Healing or the healing which is claimed to be available through methods used by Spiritism (commonly called Spiritualism). Properly understood the term emphasises the spiritual aspect of the art of healing, the truth that wholeness involves spiritual relationship with God. It should not be confused with Spiritism, and because of the possibility of such confusion, it is not entirely satisfactory.

THE CHURCH'S MINISTRY OF HEALING. The subject of this book is the Church's Ministry of Healing which primarily refers to the contribution which prayer and the sacraments make towards that wholeness which may properly be described as healing. All the means which God has put into our keeping, and which are part of the treasury of the Body of Christ as exercised through the varied gifts of healing, are included under this title.

4

PREVENTION IS BETTER THAN CURE

Seek ye first the kingdom of God, and his righteousness; and all these things shall be added unto you.

MT. 6:33.

THE work of the medical profession is more obvious and most frequently seen in its healing activities, but, as we all know, a very large part of the work of medical science is concerned with preventive medicine. Public Health services, child-welfare clinics, research in laboratories, and even statistical compilations, to mention but a few of the methods employed, are directed towards preventing disease and the conditions which breed it. Much of this work is unseen by the general public, but its effects are plain in the elimination of pestilences such as smallpox, diphtheria, and so on, which have in the past carried off millions. The study of insect life has, for example, led to methods of exterminating the carriers of plagues which have hitherto made portions of the earth's surface almost uninhabitable.

Lest it should appear that the Church's Ministry of Healing turns the Church into a sort of ambulance brigade for rescuing some of life's casualties, it is well to note that through her ministry many of the sufferings of mankind might well be prevented and eliminated.

We maintain large hospitals, rescue homes, and institutions to heal millions, while social evils producing the conditions which fill them flourish. We often hear it said that the Church should stick to religion and not meddle in politics and economics. But this is to assume that religion has nothing to do with public affairs. With that perversity which comes of thoughtlessness, the same people will demand to know why the Church does not "do something" about social wrongs. They are equally vague as to what she should do. There is an "interference" which is unjustifiable, but this does not mean that she must keep silence or that religion has no part to play in the shaping of those conditions which make for the fuller life of man. When there is abuse of political power so that human liberty and the elementary rights of men are imperilled, the Church must speak out as did the prophets of old. Whilst millions are still "displaced persons" through wars, whilst racial prejudices deprive the children of God of their inheritance, whilst bad housing conditions continue to hinder healthy family life and to produce disease, and as long as divorce and un-Christian standards of marriage result in the loss of parental love and care for thousands of children, the Church must not only raise her voice but work actively for a more Christian way of conducting the affairs of this life. She must not be content to protest, she must constructively lead the way to reform. Not to do so is to leave masses of mankind to suffer miseries and the diseases which arise from them.

In the ranks of the Church are to be found experts of all kinds whose competence to advise, direct, and influence international, national and municipal policies cannot be questioned. Inspired by Our Lord's words, "Seek ye first the kingdom of God, and his righteousness; and all these things shall be added unto you" (Mt. 6:33) they must bring to bear upon all transactions in which in their several departments they are engaged the principles of the Kingdom. To establish a more Christian ordering of society is not only to heal present ills but to prevent their recurrence.

It is not by pronouncements from highly-placed ecclesiastics and councils of the Church that these wrongs will be cured, but by the hard work and courage of Christian men and women. Great names of the past such as Shaftesbury, Elizabeth Fry, and Livingstone, remind us of what can be done. Teachers, economists, politicians, municipal councillors, doctors, nurses, indeed everyone in his capacity needs to see himself or herself as fulfilling a Christian vocation to establish the Kingdom of God in the world. The Church in action is every man active to promote Christ's sovereignty in the ordering of our common life.

Secondly, do we consider sufficiently the effect of the Christian discipline in preventing disease, whether of body or mind? Do we yet realise how the Christian way of life, the Christian way of thinking, the Christian virtues, produce that wholesomeness which immunises the individual against the assaults of both mental and physical disease? There are more people slimming for the good of their physical appearance than fasting for the sake of the body and soul together.

"Negative forces such as fear, resentment, jealousy, indulgence, and carelessness play no small part in the level of both personal and national health."[1] Here is a pointer which should indicate the part which the Christian way of life has to play.

"Train a child in the way it should go" had at one time a moral and spiritual significance, but it has come to mean in many instances that we give the child a good schooling and a start on a career that will produce a satisfactory income, and there the matter is left. "I do not believe in teaching my children religion. I think they should be left to make up their own minds when they are old enough to decide for themselves." What nonsense is this? Are we to keep from our

[1] Statement of the British Medical Association, 1947.

children the greatest influence in character-making, are we to leave unsatisfied their instinct for worship, are we to keep them in ignorance of the real meaning of sin and show them no way of salvation, and then expect them to have anything upon which to make up their minds? What anchorage is there for children brought up like this when the turbulence of adolescence comes to them and the storms of life descend upon them? How foolish it all is; no wonder that the courts are trying to mend young lives and the probation officers are kept busy!

Man is a lonely creature unless he realises that he is a social animal who must find himself in a fellowship. The diseases arising from loneliness are many. The Christian Fellowship not only provides companionship, it offers ideals of service in which preoccupation with self is obliterated, objectives worthy of endeavour in the company of others, and the outward-looking activity of worship. The alternative is likely to be a hedonistic approach to life. "Thoroughgoing hedonism," wrote Dr. William Brown in *Science and Personality* "is the worship of oneself. If it is to be called a religion it is simply the religion of extreme narcissism or self-love." This kind of worship must eventually lead to despair.

"Even if religion is a drug," wrote Beverley Nichols, "it seems to be a rather more effective drug than the average atheist can purchase from the average apothecary." There are people, of course, who treat religion as a drug, but the Christian knows the companionship of the Holy Spirit not as a drug but as the presence of the Giver of Life. With Him he finds not only solace and strength when life is difficult, but inspiration to achieve the highest and noblest, the power to realise the divinity within himself, the guiding star Who leads him to a goal that is worthy of pursuit. True and healthy religion leads the individual outwardly from himself towards an object that is worthy of his strivings, or as the Christian would say, it leads him to worship of God, and in worship he finds fulfilment.

Man can only find health of body and soul if he is properly adjusted to his environment. His environment is both physical and spiritual. It is necessary, then, that the Church should be concerned with man's material and spiritual environment as well as with his adjustment to it. In striving to bring about an improvement in the conditions under which men must live and in leading men to realise the spiritual power that is available to them in becoming adjusted to the demands which life makes upon them, the Church is engaged upon a work which is in the highest sense preventive of those ills that rob so many of peace and health.

5

HEALTH AND RELIGION

Wilt thou be made whole?
JN. 5:6.

HEALTH means two things: (*a*) that the organs in our physical body together with our mental and spiritual faculties are working together harmoniously; (*b*) that body, mind and spirit are satisfactorily adjusted to their environment. To use a word frequently found in the New Testament, it is "wholeness". But to understand what is meant by wholeness we must first understand the nature of man.

Man, like other animals, has a body. He also is possessed of mental capacity to a degree not found in the most intelligent of the lower animals. Above all, he has a spiritual perception which is not found in any other creature on earth. This is expressed in the words, "And the Lord God formed man of the dust of the ground, and breathed into his nostrils the breath of life; and man became a living soul" (Gen. 2:7). The term 'soul' is all-inclusive of body, mind and spirit, but for convenience in analysing the nature of man we use the terms 'body', 'mind' and 'spirit'. This does not mean that these parts of a human being can be found by dissection, as it were, as the organs of his body might be. The body is visible and can be weighed and measured, but the mind and the spirit are those intangible and invisible parts of us which use the body as the instrument through which they can express themselves. Nevertheless, these parts of us are so interwoven that they cannot be separated during our earthly existence.

We can liken a human personality diagrammatically to a triangle. The component parts of a triangle are essential parts of the whole figure. But imagine one side of a triangle to be bent, and the consequent distortion of the whole figure, and you have a rough picture of what happens to man's nature when some part of him is sick. His whole being is, as it were, out of true. No single part of him can be affected without the whole being in some degree affected. Whether we are sick physically, mentally, or spiritually, the whole balance of our being is upset. This may arise from stresses within or from without, or, indeed, by a combination of both.

It may not have occurred to us that the principal seat of the disturbance is sometimes, perhaps often, in the spirit. If that were not so, it might reasonably be argued that religion can have little or nothing to do with health. But when we are unsuccessfully adapted to our spiritual environment, that is to say, when we are out of tune with God, our whole being can suffer damage. Doctors who deal with the relations between body and mind have discovered and demonstrated how greatly the body is affected by the mind, and they use this knowledge in their treatments. We can carry the investigation still further and see how both body and mind can be profoundly disturbed by sickness of the spirit.

It is a well-established fact that such things as pride, jealousy, envy and hatred, to name but a few of what the Christian calls sins, are productive of ill-health. That is not to say that all sickness is due to personal sin, but it does mean that no small amount of sickness arises from such causes. Doctors have long been aware of the positive value of faith, hope, and love, and of the destructive effects of those things which flourish in their absence.

It is a commonplace for the Christian to say that Jesus came to redeem men. But do we realise that this redemption includes the body and mind of man? Why else should Our Lord have given so much time and attention to healing physical and mental sickness as well as to preaching the remission of sin? Why also did He commission His disciples to continue the healing work after His Ascension? Surely the answer is because it is the Father's will that His sons and daughters should be whole in body, mind and spirit.

Moreover, we should note that the Christian way of life, with the discipline it entails, puts us in the way of that wholeness which is true health. We recall the words of Jesus, "I came that they may have life, and may have it abundantly" (Jn. 10:10). That life is to pulse through every part of our being. It is God's will that we should be whole. Although He can use times of sickness to recall us to Himself, He does not deliberately afflict us with disease. Jesus never stretched out His hand to strike anyone down with plague; He constantly put it forth to heal.

So, if a Christian really believed that it was God's will that he should suffer sickness, he could not send for the doctor, for to do so would be contrary to what he believed to be the fulfilment of God's will for him. But if he believes that God intends that he shall be made whole, he will send not only for the doctor but also for the priest, so that he may receive every possible help that God has provided for his need.

PART TWO

6

SPIRITUAL GIFTS

> Now concerning spiritual gifts, brethren, I would
> not have you ignorant.
>
> I COR. 12:1.

IN the twelfth chapter of the first Epistle to the Corinthians St. Paul writes of the gifts God has bestowed upon
the members of Christ's Mystical Body, the Church. He
looks upon the great variety of abilities to be found among
these members, and sees them as spiritual gifts for the carrying
out of God's purposes in His Kingdom. These gifts are in the
nature of special individual endowments, but the efficiency
of the whole body is secured through the due performance by
each member of his or her office and duty. So some have a
gift for teaching, some for direction and administration, some
for preaching, some for languages, some for various kinds
of healing work, some even for the working of miracles,
and so on. Thus we see that these gifts which are dis-
tributed among the members of the Church are to be used
within the unity of the body, not merely for the good
of the Church itself, but for the mission which it has to the
world.

We are here concerned with the gifts of healings, and the
plurals are important to note as suggesting distinctions.
A study of Christ's methods of healing shows that He used

various means: words, touch, absolution, and even the application of material things like saliva and clay. In the treasury of the Church are varied gifts of healing which are applicable to the several specialised needs of particular kinds of sickness. Many of these gifts are doubtless to be looked for amongst doctors, nurses, physiotherapists, and so on. These people have special skills which have been trained and developed often to a high degree, and the Christian man or woman who possesses such abilities will regard them not merely as a means of earning a livelihood but as a vocation in which God's Kingdom may be served. The fact that these gifts have been guided and directed by scientific training does not make them less but rather more valuable, as being dedicated to the service of God by the mind as well as by the heart.

In addition to these trained gifts are those which seem to be natural endowments. For example, there are people who have a certain sympathy and understanding which enables them to render help to the mentally perplexed and unstable, or there are those who are peculiarly gifted at reconciliation. It should be remembered that many illnesses are the result of unhappy human relationships in which persons in the last mentioned category can give valuable help.

Then there are others who are endowed with that special gift of healing by touch. Spiritual gifts of this kind are termed 'charismatic'. Many instances of charismatic healing are found, but too often it is not recognised as a gift of God and so it is not offered for dedication. This particular ability is liable to go astray unless directed and submitted to the authority of the Church, but where it is found and reasonably established as authentic, there would be a good case for bringing it to the notice of the Bishop of the diocese who could give the necessary direction. In some cases this has been done, and a commission has been given for the person concerned to work under the direction of an experienced and competent director.[1]

It is sometimes asked whether the gifts of healing were withdrawn after the Apostolic age. History shows that they were not, although in later times they seem to have almost disappeared except in the lives of the saints and other holy persons. It would seem that the gifts are still present in abundance, but that so little thought has been given to the subject that they frequently go unrecognised. Undoubtedly, the effective use of them demands personal dedication, and power is increased by sanctification.

The charismatic gifts in the Apostolic period were regarded as evidences of the power of the Holy Spirit at work in the Church "dividing to every man severally as He will." The Apostles were scrupulously careful to deny any personal merit in the exercise of this power (cp. Acts 3:12; 14:8-18) and ascribed it to the risen Lord using them as His instruments. They were mindful of the words of Jesus: "Without me ye can do nothing" (Jn. 15:5). but were at the same time conscious of great power, as St. Paul said, "I can do all things through Christ which strengtheneth me" (Phil. 4:13).

Within the discipline of the Church these gifts may be safely employed, but there are many people to-day claiming healing powers whose methods and practices are, to say the least, unreliable. Recourse to them is attended by grave dangers both to faith and health. It is always an unwelcome duty to criticise others whose intentions may be sincere, whose desire to alleviate human suffering is real, but whose teachings and practices may endanger both soul and body. Church-folk will be well advised not to seek outside their own Church what can be found within it.

But the Church's Ministry of Healing is not confined to

[1] E.g. Mrs. Noel Heath in the diocese of Salisbury and Miss Helen Noble in the diocese of Manchester.

those who have a special gift of healing. Indeed, if that were so, her healing work would be seriously limited by reason of the comparatively few persons who are charismatically endowed. From the earliest times we find that this charismatic ministry, as it is called, was exercised under the sanction and, to some extent, under the control of the Bishop, and although it sometimes led to ordination it did not invariably do so, nor is it a qualification *per se* for ordination to-day. An ordained minister of the Church may be possessed of a charismatic gift which would be personal to himself and not conferred upon him by ordination, yet priests, whether so endowed or not, take a part in the healing ministry. The priest is the dispenser and guardian of the sacraments, and, as we shall see later, healing also comes through the sacraments.

We should also notice that St. Paul mentions the working of miracles as separate from the gifts of healings. This is a distinction which we shall have occasion to examine more closely, but it will suffice at this stage to observe that not only is "the working of miracles" a gift of wider application than to healing, but also that the exercise of the healing gift does not always, nor necessarily, involve the working of miracles.

So we conclude that the Ministry of Healing in the Church includes those special gifts with which some individuals are endowed, together with a sacramental ministry in the keeping of the ordained ministers of the Church, but all are included in the treasury of the Church to be used within the unity of the Body of Christ; for they are all part of the redemptive action of Christ Who has committed to the Church His power of saving both soul and body.

We should note, however, that although many of the gifts mentioned by St. Paul appear to be natural—for example, the gift of teaching—it is not only that they originate in God but that they are directed to a spiritual objective that makes them in the true sense spiritual gifts. The gift of teaching is not merely the ability to teach the three Rs, but undoubtedly has special reference to the teaching of the faith; "administrations" is not merely the gift of organising, but of administering the things of God; "nursings" or "helps" is not simply applying the techniques of medicine, but assisting in all that goes to the making of spiritual and physical well-being; and similarly, "healings" must be taken to apply to the gifts which are employed with intent to bring wholeness and not simply physical relief, and in the New Testament are independent of medical knowledge and training. The passage in 1 Corinthians 12 will be misunderstood unless we interpret it as meaning that all special gifts which are bestowed upon individuals are to be accepted from and offered back to the Giver for the fulfilment of His purpose. In short, faith and works must go hand in hand, and the powers which we have received must be dedicated to the service of God. The *charismata* are gifts of the Holy Spirit through which the Church brings God's redemptive action in Christ to those who will accept the salvation He offers.

7

THE PART OF THE LAITY

But to each one is given the manifestation of the
Spirit to profit withal.

I COR. 12:7.

THE revival of the Ministry of Healing in the Church
was brought to the attention of the general public by
the activities of certain lay "healers", the best known
at the time being the late Mr. James Moore Hickson. There
have been others since who have received the Church's
recognition of their gift of healing, but besides them there
are many who have no connection with the Church and who
employ methods which are doubtful.

As a result of the publicity which these "healers" have
obtained, there has been grave danger of the whole healing
ministry being brought into disrepute. The general public
cannot distinguish between the true and the false. Moreover,
the prominence given to the lay-healer, even when recognised
and encouraged by the Church, tends towards the idea that
the Ministry of Healing is confined to such specially gifted
persons. Such is by no means the case. Some direction is
needed as to the recognition and authorisation of lay persons
who undoubtedly have a special gift, and as to the particular
place they occupy in the ministry.

Every lay person in the Church has a real part in the
Ministry of Healing, each according to his or her gift, but
particularly and generally in the work of prayer.

In every parish there should be a prayer-group who will

make it their special work to pray, both in the group when it meets, and in their private prayers, for the sick and all who attend upon them. The importance of such a group cannot be over-estimated. The group should be properly organised with a leader who will be responsible for preparing a list of sufferers needing the prayers of the Church, and who will keep in touch with those who are prayed for and report regularly about them. Of the ways in which the prayer-group may carry out this invaluable work of intercession more is written in Chapter 13.

Another very practical form of service which the laity can render is to inform the parish priest at once of cases of sickness in the parish. It is seldom realised how difficult it is for the parish priest to know of these, especially in places where the population is large. Every conscientious priest gives priority in his visiting to the sick, infirm, and aged, and many priests working single-handed are hard pressed among the many duties they are called upon to perform. Information brought to them greatly assists them in doing what is most urgent at the right time.

Personal service to the sick and infirm is also most valuable. In country villages one sees much neighbourliness. Meals are cooked for a family when the mother is ill, rooms are tidied up, the children are cared for, and many other little helps are given which remove a burden of anxiety. This kind of neighbourly help is a real contribution which can do much to aid the recovery of the patient.

Some sick people spend long hours alone in their homes and the visits of someone who is cheerful and friendly will do much to relieve the *ennui* which engenders depression. The parish priest may know of suitable people to whom he can entrust the work of visiting a sick parishioner and who will read to and pray with him or her. Not everyone is suitable for this more specialised type of visiting, and the parish priest will have to select those in whom he can have confidence. Lay people who have time and feel they can offer this particular kind of service should make known their willingness to the priest and be ready to work under his direction.

Visiting the sick stands high among the charitable works in which all Christian folk should share. It should be regarded as a personal service to Our Lord Himself, for did He not say, "Inasmuch as ye have done it unto one of the least of these my brethren, ye have done it unto me' (Mt. 25:40)?

We considered other kinds of ministry which the laity can perform when we studied the gifts of healings, but let no one think that because he has no special gifts, his humble offering is of no value. In the feeding of the multitude Jesus took the small offering of a little boy, a few loaves and some fishes, and through them performed a miracle. It is by readiness to help in whatever way is possible that the rich treasury of Christ's Body can be opened to reveal things old and new for the healing of His people. We are His hands and feet, and as we watch Him closely we shall find the particular way in which He can use us to do some part of His redeeming work.

There is one service which can be rendered by certain few people, namely those who have themselves suffered and won through by the grace of God. There is no worse bore than someone who is always talking about his operation, and it is easy to increase alarm by the recital of the details of an illness which one has experienced. Yet it remains true that those who have themselves passed through the valley of the shadows and can testify to the rod and the staff which comforted them and delivered them, are in a strong position to bring hope and faith to many who are still in the valley. When despair and self-pity threaten to defeat, it is he who has won the victory himself in the strength which God gave him who can show the way through. Such a person can witness humbly to what God has done for him, and when others who have had no such experience are at a disadvantage, he who has already shared the fellowship of suffering will be heard. Examples of this kind of constructive help are to be seen amongst ex-polio patients and ex-inebriates who have returned to give thanks by offering practical help and inspiration to others who are still fighting the battle that they themselves fought.

8

THE PART OF THE CLERGY

And he ordained twelve, that they should be with him,
and that he might send them forth to preach, and to
have power to heal sicknesses, and to cast out devils.

MK. 3:14-15.

Many wonders and signs were done by the apostles.

ACTS 2:43.

W E have now seen some of the ways in which the
laity can take their part in the Church's Ministry
of Healing, and it is important that we should
understand that it is a ministry of the *whole Church*. The laity
and the clergy have their respective functions, and that of the
clergy includes much of what falls to the laity plus the
administration of the sacraments.

When a bishop is consecrated he is charged amongst other
things to "heal the sick".[1] This is part of Our Lord's command
to the Apostles whose successors the bishops are. The priest
who is the bishop's delegate receives by implication this same
command, for its exercise is implicit in the sacraments and
other acts for which he receives authority at his ordination.
As we have already seen, an individual priest may have been
endowed with a special gift of healing in the same way as
some of the laity, but his participation in the ministry of

[1] See Book of Common Prayer, Form of Ordaining or Consecrating of an
Archbishop or Bishop, Charge following the act of Consecration.

D

healing is not dependent upon such a charismatic endowment.

A priest is at all times the representative and embodiment of the whole Body of Christ, the Church. The Church acts through him. That is to say, when exercising his ministry he never acts as a private individual, but as the agent or instrument of Our Lord Whose authority and commands to His Church have been committed to him in his ordination. He may hand on Our Lord's blessing, absolve the sinner, and administer such of the sacraments as have not by Church order been reserved to the bishop. The sacraments reserved to the bishop only are, of course, Confirmation and Ordination.

When called to a sick person, the priest will comfort him and seek to strengthen his faith through prayer and God's message in the Holy Scriptures. He is charged to "examine whether he repent him truly of his sins, and be in charity with all the world"[1] and the sick person is to "be moved to make a special confession of his sins".

It is obvious that, when anyone is seriously ill and especially if he be likely to die, he should make his peace with God and with his neighbours. However unsatisfactory we may think the Order for the Visitation of the Sick to be in other respects, it is sound in that provision. But whether the sickness be unto death or not, confession of sin is necessary if the grace of God is to find a way into the sick man's life, for it cannot operate in an impenitent heart, and healing power cannot flow where sin blocks its entry. The ministry of absolution, then, is relevant to healing as well as to that reconciliation with God and man which must be the approach to a holy death. Moreover, when we consider how much sickness arises from such sins as uncharitableness in its many forms, intemperance, neglect of God's claims upon us, and so on, the removal of the disturbances created by an uneasy

[1] Book of Common Prayer, Order for the Visitation of the Sick.

conscience becomes a first step in any true healing process.[1] We shall return to this subject and others in this chapter in greater detail.

Then the priest will, according to his discretion, lay hands upon the sick person with prayer that he may be healed. If the sickness is likely to be prolonged and appears to be serious, he will use the sacrament of Holy Anointing or Unction for the fortification of the entire being against the strains and stresses imposed by severe illness.

Holy Communion, too, will have a place in the sick man's need, for by it he is made one with Christ's redeeming Passion and sustained by the Life of Him Who came that we might have life and have it more abundantly.

The foregoing briefly describes the ideal of the ministry of a priest to a sick parishioner. But, of course, there are many instances in which for various reasons it cannot be followed in its entirety. In such cases the prayers of the faithful must sustain the sufferer, especially those of his own household. Therefore, the priest will be concerned especially to increase the faith of the sick person's family and to bring to the home that peace and calm in which the patient can repose and find hope and fighting power. Vicarious faith was plainly acceptable to Our Lord in many instances of healing in the Gospel.

Sometimes the relations are worried lest the priest's visit should have a frightening or disturbing effect upon the

[1] There is no worse suffering than a guilty conscience, and certainly none more harmful. It has not only psychological effects—it acts as a clog upon vitality, and has far-reaching repercussions on general health. The tremendous joy brought by forgiveness plays a correspondingly important part in causing the medical effects that I refer to. In the healing by Jesus of the paralytic, we may think that the assurance that the sins were forgiven possibly created conditions favourable to the cure that followed it. But I do not think that this psychological explanation accounts for all the facts. It seems that there is a current of physical life which is re-established on contact with God. See Paul Tournier, *A Doctor's Casebook in the Light of the Bible* (S.C.M. Press Ltd., 1954).

patient. There is no need for this anxiety if his mission be rightly understood. He comes to bring healing and help, and the priest who comes with that intent will not fail to assist the sick person in ways which will make all other remedies which may be used the more effective. Often before an operation, for example, he can lay those fears which stand in the way of success. He can restore hope and confidence by which recovery is frequently initiated. Since he comes to bring Christ the Healer and Saviour, how should it be otherwise?

Friends and relations can do much to pave the way for the priest's ministry by helping the patient to receive him as one who comes with Christ's message of God's goodwill towards him and with spiritual aid which is real to assist him not only to endure but to overcome his sickness. Therefore, do not wait until the last minute to send for your parish priest. Summon him as you would the doctor as soon as the need arises. Priest and doctor can minister to the *whole* man, and God works through them both.

PART THREE

9

FAITH AND HEALING

By faith in his name hath his name made this man
strong.

ACTS 3:16.

JESUS once said, "If ye have faith as a grain of mustard
seed". This phrase reminds us that faith is a germ which
grows, a grain of life with an immense potential. Our
Lord encourages it to grow by bestowing upon us blessings
which would seem to be out of all proportion to our readiness
to receive them. It sometimes seems quite astonishing how
little Jesus demands at the outset, and with what patience and
forbearance He accepts our feeble response. Many must have
turned to Him with nothing but a simple appeal for help, and
there were others who could not make that appeal for themselves and owed their blessings to the intercession of friends
and relatives.

In Nazareth Our Lord "did not many mighty works"
(Mt. 13:58; Mk. 6:5-6) because of hardness of heart and unbelief among the people. There is an unbelief which is un-
awakened faith. It needs but some stimulus to call forth the
faith which is dormant, and sometimes dire need provides
the stimulus. Then there is an unbelief which actively opposes.
It may spring from pride or hardness of heart. The "wise and
prudent" are self-sufficient, they do not humble themselves
to ask help from anyone. Their creed is that there is nothing

man cannot do for himself. He is clever enough without God. By knowledge, they say, man can work out his own salvation; it is a sign of weakness or ignorance to ask for Divine aid. By the advance of science men will become gods.

> "Blind unbelief is sure to err,
> And scan His work in vain."

The word 'faith' is used in many different senses even in the Bible, but it has two broad applications. In the Old Testament it is used mainly in the sense of "trust in", that is, having confidence in God's mercy, relying upon Him. Its use in this sense tends rather to passivity than activity. But in the New Testament an active element enters into it, and we find it meaning 'to believe', and especially to believe in Our Lord Himself. The Gospel is the Gospel of the Resurrection, and we find the Apostles evoking something more than a passive trust. They call men to believe in the Risen Christ, in His permanent and continuing conquest over all that is meant by death, and in the new power which flows forth from Him to all who will receive it. There is, therefore, a credal content in this word 'faith' which must not be overlooked. Peter declares that it is through faith in His Name that the lame man has been made strong.

People have faith in many things: medicines, doctors, friends, even charms, and sometimes in themselves. Faith of this kind often seems to achieve a great deal, but it is different from the faith in Christ to which we are called by Christian belief. This latter faith cannot be separated from belief in what Christ is. It was in a confession of faith made by St. Peter that Our Lord said He had found the rock upon which to build His Church. Though lesser kinds of faith may have their effects, the highest and only adequate faith is built upon the conviction that in Christ God is redeeming us, and that through Christ the power of God goes forth into our lives to renew us. But unless Jesus is what He proclaimed Himself to be and what the Church teaches that He is, He is no more than any other person in whom we might say we have faith. It would seem, then, that an adequate faith must embrace some conviction about Our Lord's divinity. We trust Him for His love and sympathy, for His goodwill towards us, for His wisdom being daily proved to us, but more than all this is the life and power which flows forth from Him. That Jesus is the Son of God in the sense of the Church's creed is fundamental, and we find the Apostles stoutly denying that they have any power to heal except the power of the Risen Lord using them as channels.

It is important to remember this, for no healing can come except it comes from God, and to think of "faith-healing" as if healing came through our own psychological concentration upon it is to rest upon our own resources. It is this mistake which leads many people to attribute their failure to be healed to their own lack of faith.

Yet it must be acknowledged that many who came to Jesus for healing cannot have had a belief in His divinity as later taught and defined in credal statements about it. Such faith in Him as they were able to have was accepted and re-warded. But our faith to-day is more enlightened, for we know Him as the conqueror of death, and it is in His supreme power over all evil that we look to Him as our deliverer.

'We should not believe in "faith-healing" ' wrote Stanley Jones in *Christ and Human Suffering*, 'but Divine healing by faith—we must not believe that faith heals mental and spiritual suffering, but rather that it links us to the resources of Divine life that heals us.' The resources of Divine life are found in Him Who is Lord and God and was incarnate among us. We are not healed by some system of New Thought, nor by the enlightened spirits of departed mortals, but by the power of God in Christ. No doctrine but this will fit into the teaching of the New Testament.

This power is often brought to us through human beings whom God chooses to use, through prayer, and through sacraments, but however mediated, it is the power of God in Christ. However this power is conveyed to us, we must not mistake the means for the source. Whether we receive it through the skills of doctors, or through some form of 'religious' ministration, it is the Living Touch of the Risen Christ which we must recognise, and in recognising it we declare our faith.

So there comes into our faith an active response to the life of Christ working within us. This power does not always work with instantaneous effect, but often gradually. So our active response is shown in perseverance, in patience, as we make, perhaps, a slow progress towards health. It is called forth as we make an escape from hopeless invalidism to a hopeful and joyful recovery, as we do our part to overcome disabilities and obstacles which once seemed insurmountable. Our readiness to receive the sacraments, to pray and to act upon God's word, are parts of this active response too.

This is not the place for a theological discussion of faith in its several meanings, but rather of its practical application. Faith may be arrested at the stage which enables us to recognise God as the author of all physical phenomena. This is an intellectual appreciation of His power in the realm of nature, an acknowledgement that He is able to control physical processes, to repair and renew what has suffered damage in our bodies. But we need to go much further than this. He must come to be known to us as He who cherishes and loves us, and is willing and waiting to respond to our need of love and forgiveness when we turn to Him. As we have said, faith must be a growing reliance upon the love and goodwill of God towards us, as manifested in and mediated through

Jesus Christ His Divine Son. But the obstacle to this kind of faith is fear, and the opposite of fear is hope.

Fear is the anticipation of defeat by some evil or trial or situation, and it is the greatest enemy of health. I have heard it described as a spiritual poverty. It raises a wall which appears to be unscalable, but as the Psalmist wrote, "with the help of my God I shall leap over the wall" (Ps. 18:29*b*). We pray in the Second Collect for Peace in the Order for Morning Prayer: "that we, surely trusting in thy defence, may not fear the power of any adversaries". This is a prayer for deliverance from fear, for fear renders us powerless, and *fear itself*, not *the thing to be feared*, has the greatest power to destroy. A fearful imagination can paint a picture which is far worse than the reality, but however difficult that which is in prospect may prove to be, the Christian can be sure that he will have strength to meet it when the time comes, if he will but put his hand into the hand of Him Who has already passed that way. If we can do that, faith conquers fear and leads us on to hope. In this way faith becomes "the substance of things hoped for, the evidence of things not seen" (Heb. 11:1).

Fear bogs us down in the present so that we cannot see beyond the forebodings of the future, but faith with hope carries us into a future which is assured in the presence of Him Who has conquered the worst this world could do to Him and waits to share His victory with us. "Though I walk through the valley of the shadow of death, I will fear no evil: for thou art with me; thy rod and thy staff comfort me"; so in any trial we can go on to say with faith, "Thou shalt prepare a table before me against them that trouble me" (Ps. 23:4-5*a*).

If this kind of faith is reached, it need not be feared that it will be lost if healing does not come, for it will bring a knowledge of Christ and a strength which will carry the sufferer through to a spiritual victory, and this is more than enough.

It is cruel to attribute the absence of healing to a lack of faith on the sufferer's part, and often nothing could be less true. Nevertheless, it must not be forgotten that active faith makes certain demands upon us. For example, faith is proved by obedience. The lepers were told to go and show themselves to the priests. The nobleman was told, "Go thy way; thy son liveth", and without demanding a sign he went. The man at the pool had waited for years for the troubling of the waters, but on being told, "Rise, take up thy bed, and walk", he did so. In these and many other instances faith is proved by obedience.

Faith is also proved by perseverance. There may be difficulties to overcome. The classic examples of this come readily to mind. The woman of Canaan was rebuffed to begin with; but she continued to urge her request and was rewarded. The two blind men followed Jesus with their cries, although He went on walking away from them; they pursued Him into a house and even then were asked, "Believe ye that I am able to do this?" They came away seeing. The woman who pressed doggedly through a crowd to touch his robe, was healed. She heard some of the most gracious and tender words ever recorded, "Daughter, be of good comfort".

But the healing of a bodily infirmity is relatively a small thing. Although Jesus was glad to release men from disease, He gave a warning. It is better, He said, to enter into heaven maimed than to have all our physical powers and lose our souls. So we must expect that, when simple faith is rewarded, it will be but the beginning of a revolution in our life. He will enter into the whole of life and claim us entirely. There was another warning, "Sin no more, lest a worse thing befall thee" (Jn. 5:14). We are created in the likeness of God and we are not restored to His blue-print design merely by being rid of a physical or mental sickness. Our sanctification is a much greater thing than physical cure. The lesser may be contained in the greater, but Christ wills above all to sanctify us. So faith may begin by expecting little, but it will end by both giving and receiving all.

10

PENITENCE AND HEALING

Son, be of good cheer, thy sins are forgiven.
MT. 9:2.

IN the Order for the Visitation of the Sick, as we have
already noted, the priest is charged to move the sick
person to a special confession of his sins. The whole
tenor of this Order suggests that the sickness is liable to a
fatal termination. Taking into consideration the period in
which it was composed, a period when the death-rate from
disease must have been very high, this is not surprising.
There is also a plain implication that sickness is a "visitation"
from God, and this too emphasised the urgency of reconciliation with God. Our belief about the relationship of God
to disease is now very much changed, and scarcely any priest
to-day would be happy to use the Order, nor can one feel
that any sufferer would be the better for it. Nevertheless, the
exhortation to confession remains as the one sound piece of
pastoral advice, not only because of the possibility of death
but also because of its relevance to recovery.

It would be untrue to attribute all sickness to the sin of the
sufferer. Although we are all sinners, there are many sick
people whose lives are lived with great devotion and a constant attitude of penitence. Of such we should hesitate to
say that their sickness was the direct result of their own sin.
The human race is sinful and we are all in some measure
responsible for communal and social wrongs which entail
suffering for the innocent as well as for the guilty. On the

other hand many ailments are closely related with some spiritual disorder, and sometimes it is plainly evident that the sufferer's own sin is the cause of his condition. There is a "sin unto death", a death which involves the body along with the soul. It may be the case that the sick person is unaware of the part sin plays in the causation of his malady, or he may be secretly and grievously troubled in his conscience.

A wise and experienced physician may perceive an underlying soul-sickness as an element in his patient's illness and take such steps as he can to deal with it. But as a doctor he is not expected to convince his patient of sin or spiritual maladjustment, and an attempt to do so might be deeply resented. Moreover, should he succeed he cannot pronounce the forgiveness which brings peace and removes the sense of guilt. We may be very thankful that there are many doctors whose care for their patients extends far beyond their physical ailments and whose treatment takes full cognisance of the mental and spiritual factors involved. Their advice is often of the greatest value, and they are most likely to recognise that the skilled spiritual physician is as necessary to the patient's recovery as any service they themselves can render. Some of them would not hesitate to recommend that the patient should seek the help of the priest.

In the first Exhortation in the Order for the Administration of Holy Communion is a passage which reveals the wisdom of the Church: "that by the ministry of God's holy Word he may receive the benefit of absolution, together with ghostly counsel and advice".

It would be a gross misunderstanding of the significance of penitence and the confession it entails, if we regarded it as merely a species of psychotherapy, but it would be equally unfortunate to overlook the psychotherapeutic value of the unburdening of the conscience, of absolution, and of "ghostly counsel and advice". More sickness could be avoided than is cured, if the unhealthy conditions of mind and spirit from which so much of it springs were dealt with by the competent spiritual physician. This has been clearly indicated in the Statement issued as a Supplement of the *British Medical Journal*, 8 November 1947, which said, "Health is more than a physical problem, and the patient's attitude both to illness and to other problems is an important factor in his recovery and adjustment to life. Negative forces such as fear, resentment, jealousy, indulgence, and carelessness play no small part in the level of both personal and national health."

The late Bishop Kenneth Kirk in his book *Some Principles of Moral Theology* (Chapter IX) says that the special qualifications demanded of a spiritual director are (*a*) a father's love, (*b*), a teacher's authority, (*c*) a judge's equity, and (*d*) a physician's skill. The pronouncement of absolution, in which priestly authority derived from Our Lord is exercised, leaves no room for doubt as to the truth and reality of forgiveness, but in the healing of the soul the "ghostly counsel and advice" calls into action the qualities mentioned above. These attitudes on the part of the priest having the care of mentally or morally sick people, as well as of those who manifest no obvious signs of ill-health, will enable him to deal adequately with those underlying factors which, as the above Statement suggests, contribute to so many forms of maladjustment and actual sickness. It is in providing for this that the Church has not only shown her wisdom and understanding of souls, but has put into the hands of her clergy, alongside the authority of absolution, a function which is in the deepest sense a healing ministry.

It is not sufficiently understood how closely a man's spiritual and mental states are connected with his physical processes. Certain disorders are classified as psychosomatic. That means that they are bodily disorders which arise mainly from some psychological or spiritual maladjustment. For example, anxiety and stress arising from a troublesome business or domestic situation will give rise to a duodenal ulcer. The usual physical treatments by dieting and so forth may afford a large measure of relief, but as long as the anxiety remains there will be no permanent healing.

Penitence is a conscious desire to overcome one's recognised personal faults and sins which prevent free communion with God and obstruct one's right relationships with others. These faults and sins cannot always be properly seen and realised without the help of a spiritual expert, just as the causes of a headache cannot be properly diagnosed except by a good physician. It becomes, then, an essential part of penitence to submit oneself to this diagnostic examination and to follow conscientiously the treatment offered. It is a legal maxim that a man cannot be a judge in his own cause, for reasons which should be obvious. Similarly we can rarely make a true diagnosis of our own mental and physical states nor of our true spiritual condition. The person who is really penitent will humbly submit himself to one who can help him to know himself better and find his way to spiritual health. The humble submission of oneself to God and His will for us must involve penitence at all times of our lives. The barrier of self-will must be lowered before Christ's healing power can reach into the depths of our being. Whether we have sinned deeply or not, we are sinners who must acknowledge our frailty and weakness. Not to do so is to commit the basic sin of pride.

The word "Absolution" means "a setting free". That is exactly what is effected when a penitent soul comes to God for pardon and grace. Weakened though he may be and needing much help to recovery, he is nevertheless free from the conscious or even scarcely realised burden of guilt which has brought in its train an accumulation of ills. The right relationship with God is established, and grace to persevere is available to him. There may follow a period which is similar to that of convalescence, and progress towards spiritual well-being may well be accompanied by mental and physical improvement. This is the healing which may be properly called spiritual healing.

In the Anglican Communion the method known as auricular confession has always been regarded as a voluntary act. It has never been denied that forgiveness is freely given by God to the sincere penitent who approaches Him directly. But Christ Himself committed the power to absolve sinners to His Apostles, and the certainty which the word of Absolution gives, as well as the help of the "ghostly counsel and advice" which may accompany it, are benefits which should be carefully considered by those whose consciences are deeply stirred.

There is a prayer used by the Guild of St. Raphael which puts into words the order of progress towards that state in which God's healing power can work in us. It asks that all sick people may be led to "true penitence, full pardon and perfect peace".

11

THE LAYING ON OF HANDS
AND HOLY UNCTION

They shall lay hands on the sick.
MK. 16:18.

Anointed with oil many that were sick.
MK. 6:13.

A<small>T</small> the end of St. Mark's Gospel we read that our Lord made a promise shortly before His Ascension: "They shall lay hands on the sick, and they shall recover." Jesus was speaking to the Eleven, but He is referring to "them that believe". Faith in Him, in His promise, and in His power, will confer on those who have it certain protections and the ability to heal the sick. Also, by implication, the promise is to the afflicted who shall look to Him for aid. But there is a statement in the passage which points out that this saving power can come only to those who believe and are born anew by baptism. Those who will not accept Him cannot be saved and cannot be healed.

This appears a "hard saying", but it is true. Without faith we are without hope. Both faith and hope are psychologically necessary for healing. But it means more than that. Surrender to our Lord and His claims upon us frees us from fear and the power of sin, and sets us on the road to a new life in Him. Taking us as we are He will "sow the seed of eternal life in our hearts". So we can begin the growth of the life in grace, and that growth is towards health or wholeness. To be 'in a

E

state of grace' means that we are now on His side and that we have His help in our persevering contest with every kind of evil.

Before receiving the Laying on of Hands we must, so far as we are able, make this surrender. It means setting aside self that Christ may take command in us. There may be reasons why a seriously ill person cannot do this consciously. He may be unconscious or so weak that he cannot make any conscious effort about anything. It is then that the faith of his friends will avail him.

Nevertheless, from the earliest times of the Church's history the benefits of healing were not withheld from the unbeliever, and many accepted Christ Whom they came to know through His healing power. This should warn us not to be too rigid in our requirements as to faith, for faith may well be kindled if the unbelief is of the nature of ignorance rather than an active opposition or resistance. The healing work in mission-hospitals, for example, is evangelistic in purpose and is not limited to the converted. It is done in the name of Christian love, and in all healing work the discretion of the minister must be exercised in the spirit of Christian charity, for healing is a manifestation of God's love towards the needy rather than a reward to the righteous. The classic instance of this is seen in St. John 9 where the blind man was brought to know Our Lord by the benefit he had received from Him. This was doubtless true of a large number to whom Our Lord and His disciples ministered.

How shall a sick person obtain the Laying on of Hands? As we have already remarked, there are some people to whom God has committed a special gift of healing through touch. But they are few and the sick are many. Must the sick person wait until someone with this gift can be found and brought to him? Mercifully, no. All the clergy who have been ordained to minister the Word and the sacraments can bring

THE LAYING ON OF HANDS AND HOLY UNCTION 53

this healing touch to the sick. Send for your parish priest. He has this power from Our Lord by virtue of Christ's own commission. There is no magic in it. He brings the touch of Christ which he himself received when the Laying on of Hands was made upon him at his ordination. "As the Father hath sent me, even so send I you," Jesus has said to him. So to receive your parish priest is to receive Our Lord Himself through His ambassador.

The healing may come gradually and slowly, but let the blessing of peace flow over you, and you will soon know that God is fighting *with* you. The sick man has his own fight for health to make, but he is not making it alone. I have seen the turning-point in many an illness reached when Christ's healing touch has come to the patient. I have also seen lost faith re-born.

What will the priest do when he comes? He is directed in the Order for the Visitation of the Sick to say on entering a house, "Peace be to this house and to all that dwell in it." That is a beautiful salutation from the Prince of Peace. It reminds us of that deep harmony which prevails where people live in true love with each other and in unity with Our Lord. This peace is a vital element; where family relationships are strained or upset for any reason, there is a tension which hinders the patient's recovery, and an atmosphere inimical to that repose which is essential to healing. It is incumbent upon all members of a family to be reconciled to each other and to God. Much illness is directly caused by quarrels, grudges, and the failure to forbear with each other's faults and weaknesses. Health cannot flourish where bad relationships exist.

If the sick person is able to talk with him, the priest will ask that they should be left alone so that he may give counsel and perhaps absolution to the patient. There may be worries and sins about which the patient wishes to speak to him

privately or under the seal of confession. The relatives should
not feel hurt when they are asked to retire from the sick
room. Later he may recall them, so that they may share in
the prayers which will be offered.

So finally the priest will pray with and for the sick member
of the family, and laying his hands upon his head will say
one of the following prayers or something similar and with
the same meaning:

The grace of the Lord Jesus flow forth upon thee for the healing
of thy soul and mind and body, as we now lay hands upon thee
in His most holy Name.

or:

In the Name of God most High, may release from the pain be
given thee, and thy health restored according to His holy will.
In the Name of Jesus Christ, the Prince of Life, may new life
quicken thy mortal body. In the Name of the Holy Spirit, mayest
thou receive inward health, and the peace which passeth all
understanding.

And the God of all peace Himself sanctify you wholly; and
may your spirit and soul and body be preserved entire, without
blame at the coming of Our Lord Jesus Christ. *Amen.*

This second prayer is taken from a form of service which
he will use in its entirety if circumstances permit. Should the
patient's condition be critical or should he be too weak to
endure the complete form, the priest will use a briefer form.
But the intention will be the same.

After this, the sick person should be left quietly to make his
thanksgiving, if he is able to do so. The members of the
household should also endeavour to observe a short time of
quiet before resuming their necessary duties, and should use
it to pray for the sick member of the family, remembering,
as they do so, that their prayers are joined to those of the
whole Church. Never wrestle with God as if He were

unwilling to answer or as if your prayers must make a long journey to reach Him. He is already present in the house and never fails to bless when we humbly ask in faith, but His blessing is not always first manifested in bodily renewal. There may be a waiting time, and sometimes He heals by taking those He loves from the infirmity of the flesh to the glorified life which awaits those who have trusted Him here. There is nothing sad in death, except dying without Him.

The Laying on of Hands, then, is scriptural[1] and authorised in the Church of England. A special form of service is available through the Guild of St. Raphael, the Guild of Health, or the S.P.C.K., the last being that issued by Convocation. The clergy will also find it in a valuable pocket manual for ministrations to the sick published by the S.P.C.K. for the Guild of St. Raphael—*The Priest's Vade Mecum*, edited by the late Dr. T. W. Crafer.

We now come to a sacrament which was at one time called 'The lost pleiad of the Anglican firmament'. In the First Prayer Book of Edward VI the Order for the Visitation of the Sick included the anointing of the sick with hallowed oil, commonly called Holy Unction. In subsequent revisions of the Book of Common Prayer it was omitted and consequently fell into general disuse in the Anglican Communion. Happily it has now been restored by a resolution of Convocation dated 6th June 1935. A form for this rite was then issued and is published by S.P.C.K. and a similar form has long been in use by the Guild of St. Raphael. It will also be found in *The Priest's Vade Mecum*.

When the Twelve Apostles returned from their mission they reported to Our Lord (Mk. 6:30), and among the things they had done was the anointing of the sick with oil (Mk.

[1] It is worthy of note that, among the various means used by Our Lord, the Laying on of Hands or some other form of touch or contact with His Person is the most frequent.

6:13). In the Epistle of St. James, probably written about twenty years after Christ's Ascension, we read: "Is any sick among you? let him call for the elders of the church; and let them pray over him, anointing him with oil in the name of the Lord: and the prayer of faith shall save the sick, and the Lord shall raise him up; and if he have committed sins, they shall be forgiven him" (Jas. 5:14-15).

It will be seen from these passages that this sacrament has a firm basis in Holy Scripture, and that it was accepted as a normal procedure very early in the Church's life. It is placed, as are the other sacraments, in the keeping of the ordained ministers of the Word and Sacraments described by St. James (5:14) as "the elders of the church". Two things are signified by this. First, that it is an act of God through His Church. Second, that it is independent, as are all the sacraments, of any special gift or endowment of the individual ministering it. In short, it is one of the covenanted 'means of grace'.

The question is sometimes asked, "What is the difference between the Laying on of Hands and Holy Unction?" The difference cannot be defined in terms of efficacy as one might differentiate between the suitability of one drug as against another. The methods of laboratory examination and experiment are not applicable to the things of the Spirit. Neither qualitative nor quantitative comparisons are relevant. Both the Laying on of Hands and Anointing with oil were used by the Apostles, but we have no clear evidence whether or why one was preferred rather than the other.

The visible acts differ: the first involves touch or direct contact which, as we have seen, was frequently employed in one form or another by Jesus; the second includes the use of a substance associated with healing as a commonly used materia medica in both Old Testament and New Testament times. But oil was also used as a means of hallowing and implied consecration. In the Old Testament we find it employed to sanctify both things and persons who thus became set apart to sacred use and service. In Christian times it has been used in connection with Baptism, Confirmation, and Ordination, and its use is continued to the present day in the Coronation Service. The anointing of a baptised person in a time of sickness may well be thought of as a re-hallowing of one whose body and spirit have been invaded by sin or subjected to assault by evil powers.

The Laying on of Hands suggests the reaching out of the Divine compassion and the establishment of contact with the Giver of Life. In this sense the Laying on of Hands has an evangelistic significance which makes its use more widely suitable than that of a sacrament which is for those whose identity with the fellowship of the Church is more firmly established. It is not inappropriate that this sign should also accompany anointing with oil. But the sacrament of Holy Unction which carries with it the significance both of healing and of hallowing, has by tradition come to be regarded as appropriate to those whose place in the Body of Christ has been sealed by Baptism and, except in the case of a young child, by Confirmation.

Moreover, while the Laying on of Hands may be administered by a lay person possessing a gift of healing, Holy Unction as a sacrament is reserved to "the elders of the Church", that is, to the ordained ministers whose authority to be dispensers of the sacraments has been conferred upon them by ordination. In this respect both the Laying on of Hands and Holy Unction administered by a priest are independent of a charismatic gift of healing which he may or may not possess. Although there is no evidence to show that these two healing rites were ever regarded as alternatives bearing any difference in efficacy, both are used, and used frequently in conjunction, as part of the sacramental provision made by Christ and committed to those endowed by ordination with Apostolic authority.

The oil in Holy Unction is not, of course, used for its natural healing properties, but as the symbol of healing and the matter of a sacrament whereby healing, hallowing, and fortifying grace is conveyed to the sick person. It is accompanied by the cleansing of absolution and the prayers of the faithful. The oil used is pure olive oil, normally blessed by the bishop, and by tradition the stock of oil is consecrated on Maundy Thursday for use in the ensuing twelve months. If for good reason it is not possible to obtain oil hallowed by the bishop, the priest may hallow it himself. This blessing of the oil is analogous to the blessing of the water used in Holy Baptism.

Over a long period in the Church's history Holy Unction has suffered both misuse and neglect. It has been treated as a last rite for the dying with little or no thought of healing and, being administered at the very last moment, came to be associated with death rather than with healing. In our own Church it has suffered neglect more than misuse. Nevertheless, it has in recent times been restored to its proper place and use in the Anglican Communion, and should be sought and received early in any serious illness, whether acute or prolonged.

As with other healing rites, the preparation is by penitence and faith. Such preparation as is required for Holy Communion is also applicable to Holy Unction, and a particular confession should be made when the condition of the sick person allows. In other cases a simple act of contrition suffices, or in cases where the patient is quite unable to respond for himself, prayer on his behalf should be made which will express the desire for forgiveness which he cannot express himself.

He should also receive at the same time the Laying on of

Hands, and then, or at some near time, Holy Communion. The peace and strength brought to the hard-pressed soul and body of the sufferer in this way is wonderful, and sometimes healing is seen to begin from that very moment.

Holy Unction, because it is a sacrament, is restricted to those who are baptised. It is a simple act of prayer accompanied by the signing of the cross upon the forehead with oil, as is done with water at Holy Baptism. The parish priest will administer Holy Unction to those in need of it, and it should be remembered that he does not act as an individual but as the empowered and accredited ambassador of Him Who said, "I am come that they may have life and have it more abundantly."

When sickness comes with all its trials for body, mind and spirit, the fortifying influence of this sacrament cannot be over-estimated. It will often bring that added peace and strength which can turn the tide in favour of recovery. But that is not all. To all of us death must come at last, and when that great moment of liberation is at hand, Holy Unction together with Holy Communion will enable us to grasp the strong hand of our Deliverer and to pass peacefully and fearlessly with Him through the valley.

Christ has left with His Church the means of grace to bring to us that particular help we need in various states of life. In Holy Marriage there is blessing and grace given for the new life together of the married pair; in Ordination there is the endowment of grace for performing the difficult task of ministering to souls. Similarly Holy Unction is the sacrament for the special need of a person in sickness. Our Blessed Lord used various means to heal men's infirmities, even spittle and clay. Here He offers His healing love through hallowed oil and prayer. Who, desiring to be whole, will despise it? There can be no doubt that the Church of England has done well to restore this once 'lost pleiad'.

The prayer used in the anointing of the sick is as follows:

N. I anoint thee with holy oil in the Name of the Father, and of the Son, and of the Holy Ghost.

As with this visible oil thy body is outwardly anointed: So our heavenly Father, Almighty God, grant thee of His infinite goodness that thy soul inwardly may be anointed with the Holy Ghost, Who is the Spirit of all strength, comfort, relief, and gladness: and vouchsafe for His great mercy (if it be His blessed will) to restore unto thee thy bodily health and strength to serve Him; and send thee release of all thy pains, troubles, and diseases, both in body and mind; through Jesus Christ Our Lord, who by His death hath overcome death, and with the Father and the Holy Ghost evermore liveth and reigneth, God, world without end. *Amen.*

12

HOLY COMMUNION AND HEALING

Except ye eat the Flesh of the Son of Man, and drink
His Blood, ye have no life in you.

JN. 6:53.

THE Church's Ministry of Healing rests, of course,
first and last on Our Lord. The healing works of the
Apostles are all done in the Name and power of the
Risen Lord (Acts 3:16). When there is any danger that
anyone may attribute these wonderful works to the personal
power of the Apostles themselves, they sharply remind them
that Christ is the real source of the power committed to
them (Acts 3:12). It is very important to keep this truth
central in all our thought about the ministry of healing.

In Holy Communion we approach the Father through the
Son and plead Christ's sacrifice made once for all for our
redemption. All the power of God goes forth through the
Son to keep us back from the power of evil working to
possess us in body, mind, and spirit. "Except ye eat the flesh
of the Son of man and drink His Blood, ye have no life in
you" (Jn. 6:53). and this we do in a spiritual manner every
time we devoutly receive the Sacred Elements. "The Body
. . . the Blood of our Lord Jesus Christ, preserve thy *body*
and *soul*."[1] There is no sundering apart of the physical and
spiritual here. The whole man is included in the benefits to
be bestowed in this Holy Sacrament.

[1] See Book of Common Prayer, The Communion, Words of Administration.

So St. Paul writes to the Corinthians: "For this cause many are weak and sickly among you" (1 Cor. 11:30). For what cause? Because of neglect or an unworthy receiving. The word used for "weak" means without strength, physical, mental, and spiritual, and it is reinforced by the word for "sickly" which can be translated only by "infirm" or "sick". We come into immediate contact with the creative and re-creative power of God in Christ as we humbly and penitently receive the Blessed Sacrament, and we are warned of the danger of "not discerning" (verse 29), a term which carries the meaning of "being in opposition to" or "separating oneself from". To approach that which is holy while not in a state of grace is dangerous.

These passages show how closely connected health and sickness are with the way in which we are related to God through Christ. That does not mean that we must not approach Our Lord in the Holy Sacrament until we are perfect—for that we shall never be in this life—but that, coming to Him in penitence and faith, we seek perfection of which wholeness is the ultimate reality. Therefore, in a devout reception of Holy Communion we are coming to Christ in the same way as so many did in the days when He walked this earth.

We cannot put this better than in the words we find in the Book of Common Prayer, first in the Prayer of Humble Access in the Order of Holy Communion: "We do not presume to come . . . trusting in our own righteousness, but in thy manifold and great mercies", and again in the last paragraph of the Catechism: "have a lively faith in God's mercy through Christ". So, knowing our great need, we come to Our Lord for help and for that fulness of life which He offers to us.

Now there are two answers commonly made by sick people when it is suggested to them that they should receive the

Holy Sacrament in a time of sickness. One is, "I would rather wait until I am better"; the other is, "Am I as bad (meaning ill) as all that?"

Consider the first. It amounts to a failure to see that by this very means Our Lord can come to make us better. It is like saying that you will not send for the doctor until you are well.

The second seems to mean that although we receive Holy Communion when we are in health, Christ is no longer of any use to us until we are at the point of death.

Probably the people who make these answers do not really see what is implied in them, but we should be quick to correct them in love. They are denying themselves the mercies of God at the moment when they are most in need of them.

Behind the first answer there may be, of course, a feeling that it requires a mental and spiritual effort of which they do not feel capable. But the answer to this is quite clear. That is part of the weakness which Our Lord wants to heal. He knows all about it. It is not too much to say that He has shared it and experienced it when He cried in His own terrible weakness from the Cross, "My God, my God, why hast Thou forsaken me?" God does not demand of us more than we can do. He is quick to come to our aid with His strength if we will but cast our burden upon Him. All that is necessary is to let Him come and simply to put out our hands to receive Him.

We should learn to think very simply of Christ present in the Holy Sacrament. We need to recall the days when He was here upon earth. Would you have refused to receive Him if He had knocked upon your door as He passed by? Remember the blind man sitting by the wayside (Mk. 10:46ff.; Lk. 18:35ff.). "Who is that passing by?" he asked. They told him, "Jesus of Nazareth". "How I need Him!" he must have thought, "Would He take notice of one like me?" Then he began to call out, "Thou Son of David, have mercy on me!" Jesus stood still on hearing that cry, and for the next few moments nobody else could claim His attention. When Jesus comes to us in the Blessed Sacrament it is just like that. He is there, He stands and looks upon us, He puts forth His hand to touch us. Each one of us is for the moment the sole object of His attention. Poor, blind, and helpless we may be, but that is why He stops in His journeying to look upon us.

All of this has to do with our personal need of Our Lord and His response to it. But there is also another aspect which must not be overlooked. We are members one of another in Christ. By Baptism we became living parts of His Body the Church. The Holy Communion is a corporate act of the Church. It is the great act of intercession. Everyone who is concerned for the sick members of the Church must bear them to Our Lord at the Altar. The corporate faith in which the mighty works of God can be accomplished cannot be better expressed than when we are all united in obedience to His command, "Do this in remembrance of Me."

There is also one further thought in this which we should pass on to the sick who are isolated in their homes or separated in hospital. Sickness makes us feel this apparent separation, but as the sick person receives Holy Communion the sense of isolation is removed. He is one with the whole body of the faithful and is caught up into the great company of those who are interceding for him at the Altar. Visiting days are greatly looked forward to in hospital, for by them the sick are kept in touch with home, with the love of their relatives and all that is meant by the family. Similarly, in Holy Communion the priest's visit is like a touch of home, bringing the love of the family in Christ to him.

In this corporate faith, by the solicitude and prayer of the

Family of God, and through the Life of the Redeemer entering into him, the sick man finds peace, strength, comfort,
and healing. He is, even though for the time being physically separated, in true communion with God and all the
faithful.

13

INTERCESSION

Call upon me in the day of trouble: I will deliver thee, and thou shalt glorify me.

PS. 50:15.

I

A N eminent physician once said to me, "We must not expect prayer to do more than it is meant to do." But what is prayer meant to do? We are bidden to "pray without ceasing", to pray with faith and perseverance, even with importunity. Nevertheless, the prayer of faith with all its promised power is not to be treated as if it were an Aladdin's lamp. We do not summon up God to do our bidding. By submitting our cause to our heavenly Father we can make it possible for Him to achieve His purpose. That is what prayer is meant to do. The efficacy of prayer lies in the expression of our dependence upon God, in our readiness to follow the guidance of the Holy Spirit, and to link up our human endeavours to His purpose of love. Prayer is not a human activity which by itself will achieve what man desires; it is the way by which God can act as man puts himself in right relationship with Him.

Both St. Matthew and St. Mark record Our Lord's words, "If ye have faith, and doubt not . . . ye shall say unto this mountain, Be thou removed, and be thou cast into the sea; it shall be done. And all things, whatsoever ye shall ask in prayer, believing, ye shall receive" (Mt. 21:21-22, Mk. 11:23). Similar statements are also recorded in Mt. 17:20 and Lk. 17:6. This appears to mean that the prayer of faith is almost limitless in its possibilities; but the phrase "Be thou removed" was a proverbial expression used of the solution of a difficult matter, and the implication is that no difficulties are insurmountable when we approach them in dependence upon God.

We must not, however, fasten our attention upon one aspect only of this power of prayer. When Jesus was tempted in the wilderness to turn stones into bread it was not because He had no power to do so that He refused. When He prayed in Gethsemane that the bitter cup of suffering might be taken from Him, it was not. He did not then proceed to repudiate His heavenly Father, but accepted His will. So we learn that the prayer of faith is always the prayer which seeks the fulfilment of a purpose of God. In the Lord's Prayer, "Thy will be done" comes before any petition, and the alignment, as it were, of our desires and objectives with what we come to perceive to be God's will and purpose is the ultimate proof of the prayer of faith. The prayer of faith is only possible if we can believe that God's will and purpose is the fulfilment of His love and goodwill towards us. Christ's refusal to turn stones into bread was because, humanly speaking, He perceived that God's purpose for man could not be achieved by merely material provisions, and His acceptance of the cup of suffering was because He trusted the Love that would achieve redemption for man through the suffering He must endure. The prayers of Our Lord were perfect, and praying in His Name means identifying ourselves with His attitude towards God the Father as we make our prayers.

Often we "see through a glass darkly", but as we grow in prayer our knowledge of God becomes more mature. The mother of Zebedee's sons came to Jesus to ask that they might have the chief places in His kingdom and was told, "Ye know

F

not what ye ask." St. Paul prayed for the removal of his "thorn in the flesh" but it remained, and he made the great discovery that "my grace is sufficient for thee". Prayer is not a means of forcing God's hand. That it certainly cannot do. But it can make known to Him our readiness and worthiness to receive what in His great love He is willing to give for our ultimate good. It will sometimes happen that the answer to our prayers is different from what we should have expected and from what we have asked, but it will be found to be the best. Prayer does not test God: it does test us. The will of God towards us is always good, and to that truth we must hold fast in all our praying. "If we ask any thing according to his will, he heareth us: and if we know that he hear us, whatsoever we ask, we know that we have the petitions that we desired of him" (1 Jn. 5:14-15).

Our prayer life is arrested at a very elementary stage if we confine it to petition, and we are constantly in need of repeating the request made to Our Lord by His disciples, "Lord, teach us to pray." "Minds religiously affected are wont, in everything of weight and moment which they do or see, to examine according unto the riches of piety what dependency it hath of God, what reference to themselves, what coherence with any of these duties whereunto all things in the world should lead, and accordingly they frame the inward disposition of their minds to admire God, sometimes to bless Him and give Him thanks, sometimes to exult in His love, sometimes to implore His mercy. All which different elevations of spirit unto God are contained in the name of prayer."[1]

If, then, we are asked "What is prayer meant to do?" we must reply that it is meant to bring us into closer communion with God, and as a result of this we shall learn "to ask such things as shall please Thee". We might well begin our

[1] Hooker, *Ecclesiastical Polity*, V, xlviii, 2.

petitions by praying the Collect for the Tenth Sunday after Trinity.

A sufficient basis for "prayer" [wrote Fr. Martindale][1]—what Catholics call "the raising of the mind to God"—is the simple fact that two intelligences, if in contact, can interact. God is wholly present in our souls: He cannot be unconscious of us: it remains for us to put ourselves actively into "presence" with Him. Moreover, God is active and takes all initiative in all things; in a sense, we must resist, if we do not pray: we speak of God "answering" us: it is truer to say that prayer is our answer to His endless solicitation of our mind and will.

When we pray, then, let us ask for much, and with perseverance and even importunity, for we have Our Lord's authority for doing so, and Our Heavenly Father is "always more ready to hear than we to pray" and is "wont to give more than either we desire or deserve". Moreover, He knows "our necessities before we ask, and our ignorance in asking". If what we ask is, in the sight of His wisdom and in the purpose of His love, right for us, He will grant it, but if He has a better thing for us He will give it in the right way and at the right time. Often God gives so much more than we ask, but we do not realise this all at once. There is no limit to His power and love, neither should there be a limit to our faith and patience. "The prayer of a righteous man availeth much," wrote St. James, and a righteous man is, surely, he who would be right with God.

[1] *The Faith of the Roman Church*, (Sheed and Ward, 1950).

II

Real intercession makes great demands upon us. In every place we find human sympathy. When a person is afflicted by some misfortune there is never lacking a general concern amongst his neighbours. Many more, however, will be found ready to express their sympathy in messages and even to perform charitable works than to undertake prayer on his behalf. But faith and works must go hand in hand. The service we render to our sick neighbours is defective unless we both pray for them and do what lies in our power to assist them in practical ways. To intercede truly we cannot be content with a few moments snatched from our busy lives to say a prayer or attend an intercession service. We must enter more deeply into the situation than that.

The Incarnation teaches us the meaning of prayer. God entered into our human life to share the conflict, to suffer with us, and to release us from our bondage. Praying for our neighbours requires that we emulate God, that we enter as fully as we can into their situation, suffer with them, if needs be, and use every opportunity we have to bring them relief. Compassion means bearing one another's burdens, for so we fulfil the law of Christ. Prayer calls for sacrifice, for suffering, for devotion to good causes and active participation in all efforts to relieve the miseries which are suffered by individuals.

Much of the healing work of Christ is being performed by people who have thus gone down into the abyss to rescue others. We should pray for and praise God for those Christ-like people who, to-day, give up many comforts and worldly advantages to help displaced persons, to rescue ill-treated children, to visit in prisons, to alleviate the lot of the poor and lonely, and to restore women who have fallen into sin.

Where Christian love inspires this kind of service we see intercession at its best. Some people have answered a call to devote themselves wholly to the work of prayer and have embraced the religious life in convents and monasteries.

We cannot all, of course, undertake work of that sort, but in our more limited sphere we may find scope amongst our near neighbours. Prayer means more than words and pious aspirations, and its efficacy is discovered as we put ourselves at God's disposal as fully as we can. As the saintly Bishop Weston said, "You cannot claim to worship Jesus in the tabernacle if you do not pity Jesus in the slum." The thought which must always be with us is, "Inasmuch as ye have done it unto one of the least of these my brethren, ye have done it unto Me."

If works without prayer are incomplete, so is prayer without the service that it is within our power to render. One of the difficulties which intercessors often express is that they are not able to pray for people whom they do not know or whose circumstances are not, at least in some measure, known to them. It is inevitable that we shall be asked to pray for people we cannot meet, but we could sometimes know, or know something about, many more of our fellow parishioners than we do. But the name of each person commended to our prayers is that of a child of God, and an inheritor of the Kingdom of Heaven, a person who loves, suffers, feels pain and knows fear. If we remember that, the name is no longer a few marks made on paper but a living brother or sister. It is our privilege and duty to bring each one into the Presence of Him Who knows every need and will not fail to meet it. It is not what *we* know about them that matters so much as what Christ the Healer knows.

There can be no more exalted moments of intercession than those we keep in the covenanted Presence of Christ in the Holy Eucharist. Our own local altar where, as in the case of many country parishes, only a very small company may be assembled, is really the Altar of the whole Church, so that we are not offering just the prayers of a tiny congregation but incorporating our intercessions with those of all the faithful everywhere. The Church is gathered together at the foot of the Cross to plead the Sacrifice once made for our redemption, and as we pray, "Lord, he whom thou lovest is sick, come and heal him", we know that He Who ever makes intercession for us at the right hand of the Father gathers them up into His own perfect offering. The reading of a list of names before the altar may seem dull, but if we offer it with attention and intention, it is as if we had brought a company of sick and infirm just as people did in the days of Our Lord's earthly presence in Palestine.

When Hezekiah was troubled by a threatening letter from Sennacherib he took it to the House of the Lord and spread it before the Lord. Our list of intercessions could well be left in like manner upon the altar to make its silent appeal to God as we go away to our duties elsewhere.

Every parish should have its intercession group who will make the sick in their midst their particular care. If every parish were diligent in this few sick people would be forgotten, and the organising of prayer groups at special and sometimes remote centres would not be necessary. Moreover, intercession at the parochial level enables those who pray to know, and be in constant touch with, the sick who need their prayers. The group should frequently recall the case of the paralytic brought by his friends into the presence of Our Lord (Mk. 2:3-12) for this so aptly describes what they are called upon to do. Note the words "their faith" and the perseverance with which it was put into action.

The group should meet frequently, weekly if possible, and often at the Holy Eucharist. But although there will always be some who wish to make intercession for the sick their

special offering to God, the existence of a group should not
be taken to mean that others are exonerated from the duty
of prayer for the sick. At the times of the public services the
whole congregation should be called upon. The efficacy of
our prayers does not, of course, depend upon numbers. How
unjust it would be if those who had the greatest number to
pray for them received the greatest benefits, or if those who
had but one could expect but little from God! But the
members of God's Family have a right to expect that all the
family cares.

Pray also for the doctors and nurses of the local hospital,
the local medical practitioners and the district nurses, and
above all pray for the relatives of the sick and let them know
you are doing so. If it can be arranged, let two or three gather
together to pray when the parish priest goes forth to minister
to a sick neighbour.

A prayer group should be organised in a businesslike way
with a leader or secretary who will keep the list of names up
to date and get reports about the sick at regular intervals.
Nothing can be more unreal than to go on praying without
information of this kind, and thanksgiving for recovery and
improvement should also have a definite place in the group's
activities. But persevering prayer should go on even when
there seems to be no evident result, for the ways of God are
not our ways and He may be working His purpose out in
some direction we had not thought of. Jesus told a parable
about praying and not losing heart (Lk. 18:1-8) and another
about persistence in asking (Lk. 11:5-10) and the woman of
Canaan was commended because she would not be daunted
(Mt. 15:22-28).

The simplest form of prayer is, "Lord, thy servant is sick,
come and heal him", and for some people this would be
enough, but others find it easier to pray if they know the
nature of the illness and something of the circumstances of

the case. In public prayer one must be cautious about such information. There may be good reason for a sick person being kept in ignorance of the nature of his sickness, and care must be taken that there is no leakage of the information. Furthermore, we must avoid the conclusion that the illness is of such a kind that it is hopeless to pray for recovery. Whatever the sickness may be it is not necessary to inform God about it, nor is it beyond His power to heal it, nor do we need to know in order to direct the Almighty. So details should be sparingly given, and the leader's discretion in these matters must be reliable. If it is clear that God is calling a soul through death to that final healing which awaits us all, then let prayers be said for a departing soul with no sense of failure but with the conviction that the call is God's best answer.

People who are very ill often cannot pray for themselves, so that a privilege and duty which may be accorded to us is to pray with them. These prayers should not be lengthy, but they should be full of faith and hope. The Lord's Prayer, a suitable psalm or a short passage of Scripture, or perhaps a hymn prayerfully said, can bring a complete change of atmosphere into a sick-room and a spirit of calm and confidence to the sufferer. It may be better to stand rather than kneel by the bedside, and one finds that many sick folk find comfort in the touch of one's hand upon theirs. Try to help the patient to pray so that he does not feel you are praying *at* him nor merely *for* him, but *with* him. He may be able only to struggle through the Lord's Prayer or even murmur the Amens, but you will have helped him to pray himself. There is a time when weakness is so great that no audible participation is possible, but even unconscious patients are sometimes more able to have some awareness of what is happening than we are apt to suppose.

Whether we pray in the intercession group or at a bedside,

the real purpose of our prayer is to bring the sick nearer to God that they may find in Him the strength they need in the situation as it is. The following prayer is a beautiful one which suits every occasion:

O Eternal Lord, Who art the strength of all that trust in Thee, we bring now into Thy Presence thy servant(s) . . . . We know not what is best for him, but Thou knowest. We beseech Thee to lay Thy healing hand upon him, give him all that he needs for health both of body and soul; grant unto him patience and endurance, and a perfect dependence on Thy never-failing love; and work out in him the good pleasure of Thy will. All this we ask in Thy Holy Name. *Amen.*

14

SILENCE AND MEDITATION

Be still and know that I am God.
PS. 46:10.

WE live in an age of noise and speed. The leisurely ways of our grandparents have gone for ever. The slow methods of craftsmanship are replaced by mass-production and the conveyor-belt; the jogging horse-drawn cart by the motor-car; the news of the world, whether good or bad, is brought to us with such rapidity that we have no time to digest its significance; the wireless set and the television screen bombard us with news, views, and entertainment, and form a background of sound from symphony to rock 'n roll. The effects of noise and speed, and the high pressure of modern living conditions are taking their toll. Our nerve mechanisms are given little rest and we have too many distractions to allow us to reflect. The new starvation is in the realm of the spirit rather than of the body.

Man cannot live by bread alone and the Welfare State cannot meet all his needs. Millions do not know the meaning of relaxation and live at a constant pitch of activity, and much present-day sickness is directly due to this. We need to recover the habit of relaxing and reflecting, and this can only be done by setting aside time for silence and meditation.

The "still small voice" which speaks into the heart of man can only be heard in stillness, and until it is heard our deepest needs cannot be fed with the Bread of Life. Our sense of proportion and the appreciation of true values can only be kept if we allow time for reflection and turn aside from the stridency of the noisy world in which we must pass the greater part of our time.

Silence and meditation, then, have a part to play both in preventing disease and in restoring health. The Quiet Day, the Retreat, and the self-imposed discipline of at least a weekly period of quiet withdrawal from the stream of our normal daily round have become increasingly necessary. It is a frequently heard criticism that even the liturgical services in church do not provide time for silence, and although our weekly worship with the People of God gives expression to many of our spiritual needs and aspirations, some provision for keeping quiet in the Presence of God ought to be made. The open church, of course, affords a place for quiet and meditation outside service hours, and it is worth while to form the habit of spending ten minutes or a quarter of an hour in it on the way from work or when out shopping. Many of the worries, anxieties, and confusions which do so much damage to health would be stilled if we learned how to be still and to wait upon God.

Prayer is known to many only as petition. We need to learn to pray in silent adoration, to listen to the voice of God in meditation, and to discover that God answers our petitions if we will but give Him the opportunity to speak to us. The attitude of the child Samuel, "Speak, Lord, for thy servant heareth", is all too often absent from our prayer life.

This is not the place to give instruction on how to meditate. There are little manuals and tracts, as well as larger classical works, which may be easily obtained, and which will help those who take this part of prayer life seriously. But it is necessary to make up our minds that amidst the many calls upon our time and attention, the time set aside for waiting upon God for refreshment is essential to our well-being.

But this applies not only to the preservation of health or to

recovery from illness. Intercession groups should also allow
a place for silence and meditation. The very title "Intercession Group" tends to imply that the main business of the
group is to offer petitions, and the intercession list is often
so long that there is little time for anything else. Leaders of
groups would do well to arrange for a session, at least month-
ly, when the main business would be to wait upon God in
silence and meditation under the guidance of the parish
priest. A passage of Holy Scripture might be slowly read,
some leading thought indicated by the conductor, and then
the members should be left to think upon it and pray in their
own fashion, and apply the truth discovered from it to the
purpose or problems with which they are engaged in their
intercessory work. Many of the difficulties of intercession
would find their solution if we learned of God as well as
prayed to Him in petition.

A period of silence before intercession, too, enables us to
realise that God is with us and to link our prayers with the
intercession which Our Lord is ever making for us. This kind
of approach to prayer for others may be likened to a characteristic of Jesus which is often mentioned in the Gospels.
He "lifted up his eyes to heaven", or He "looked up to
heaven", we are told, when He was about to pray or to
perform some healing work. As we are beset with so many
distractions, uncertainties, and fears, it is essential that we
escape from them by looking up to heaven where we may
see the Father and the Son awaiting us with love and compassion, with strength and assurance. Our citizenship is in
heaven; we are but pilgrims here; but we can for a time enjoy
that citizenship if we will only give ourselves to the opportunity.

I remember a minister beginning a prayer-meeting with a
fervent petition that God would come down and be with
those about to pray. It seemed to me an inversion of the real

attitude of true prayer which does not invoke a far-off God
to come down out of heaven, but recalls us to His presence
with us. "Be still and know that I am God." In this stillness
we become aware of God Who is all around and within us,
waiting to work His perfect will in us and in those for whom
we pray if we will but give Him the chance to do so. His
healing power is not something to be sought with great
difficulty but to be accepted, already at work within us but
sometimes held at arm's length by our preoccupation with
other things. His heaven, too, is not remote; it is where He
is, and therefore it is with us as we are in communion with
Him. As Jesus said, "The kingdom of heaven is within you"
or "among you", not to be reached out for but to be realised.
"Looking up to heaven" then becomes a detachment from
earthly things as we rest in the Presence of God. The practice
of the Presence of God, as Brother Lawrence taught, is the
secret of peace and security, the very essence of the
spiritual life.

It is in the prayer of Silence that we look upon God Our
Heavenly Father and discover that we are already in the
Kingdom of Heaven, in that realm in which, existing as it
does in the midst of a world where man seeks to dominate
everything by the force of his own will, God's will still
remains supreme and operative in the hearts and lives of men
of faith.

PART FOUR

15

DISEASE AND THE WILL OF GOD

> For God created man to be immortal, and made him to
> be an image of his own eternity.
>
> WISD. 2:23.

THE answer given to the problem of the will of God
in relation to health and sickness is open to over-
simplification, and it is therefore necessary to consider
it in some detail.

The general statement that disease is quite manifestly not
intended by God but that, on the contrary, He wills that all
men should be whole, that is, in full health of body, mind,
and spirit, is true and capable of proof. But on looking more
deeply into it in the light of experience one suspects that it
needs some qualification. In its simple and unqualified form
it leads many people to the conclusion that *every* case of
sickness should be healed when in fact some are not. If it
were unconditionally true, we could not pray "If it be
Thy will", and, indeed, there are many people who feel
unable to do so.

When we are confronted with instances in which the
disease and the suffering it entails remain, some sincere
Christians will say that this is due to lack of faith, to un-
repented sin, or to some other spiritual fault in the life of the
sufferer. But this is often a false and dangerous conclusion
which can produce much distress. The fact is that we see

both the saints and the ungodly flourish and sicken, and we cannot point to sufferers and say of them that they are more sinful than other men, nor can we point to the healthy and say that they are so because they are of more than average goodness. It is not possible to separate the sheep from the goats in this easy fashion, and we have to recognise that disease is indiscriminate in its selection.

A man looking upon some spectacle of human misery may be moved to say, "I would not do that to my worst enemy." If he attributes this condition to God's will, he will go on to draw one of two conclusions: either that God is more cruel and less moral than himself, or that there cannot be a God in a universe in which such things can happen. But if you challenge his argument by saying that God is a God of love and that the man's miserable state cannot be according to God's will, he will ask, "Then why does He not cure him?" It is but a short step to the further conclusion that either God does not want to do so or that He cannot. If he learns that much prayer has been offered for the sufferer, his conviction may well be strengthened. This is a situation which often arises.

The argument that disease is contrary to God's will for man is supported thus:

(a) That God made all things to be perfect and it is inconceivable that He would proceed to mar and destroy His own handiwork.

(b) That Jesus asserted many times that He came to do His Father's will, and that, so far from inflicting disease on anyone, He spent a great part of His time healing.

(c) That if we really believed that God wills men to suffer disease, we could not believe that He has inspired men to overcome it, for that would be to contradict Himself. Therefore, the science of medicine and all other efforts to defeat sickness would be contrary to God's will and purpose.

It would then be irreligious to send for the doctor or to use any means to heal anyone.

(d) That the body's natural resistance and its capacity for self-repair is evidence of the Creator's design to preserve His perfect work.

(e) That if it be granted that God is love, He could not afflict men as some think He does.

Now all this may be true, but the question remains: if disease is not inflicted by God, who or what is responsible for it?

The answer offered to this is:

(a) That it is due to our sin and ignorance; both personal and communal sins create the conditions in which disease can flourish.

(b) That this is possible because God created man with free will; human beings are free to reject God and His laws or to accept them; without such freedom we should be automata and not human beings.

(c) That this abuse of our freedom arose at the outset of human history and has continued ever since.

We are trying to solve the problem of responsibility for human suffering, and we are led to the difficulty of deciding whether it rests wholly upon man or, at least in some measure, upon God in making man a creature capable of disobedience. This leads us to the idea that God's primary will for man is health or wholeness, but that man by the misuse of God's gift of freedom frustrates the Creator's intention and involves himself in a state which God does not desire for him. Unless we deny man's moral responsibility and say that he cannot sin, and also ignore God's redemptive action through Jesus Christ, we cannot arrive at any other conclusion.

If we consider the disease which exists among animals and plants which have no free will, and the suffering caused by catastrophes such as floods, earthquakes, volcanoes and so on, we are led to the doctrine that evil spiritual agencies had already rebelled against God before the world began, and have retained a limited and temporary power of creating disorder in the Universe. Man has succumbed to the influence of these spiritual beings and has become susceptible to their disordering and destructive power. This is known as the doctrine of a pre-cosmic fall.

Some people find a difficulty in this teaching, which at first sight appears to involve a dualism. But a dualism can only exist where there are two gods, not between the One Uncreated God opposed by some of his own creatures. The belief that there are fallen angels capable of resisting the Creator and thereby spreading discord and destruction in the cosmos no more involves a dualism than the evident fact that man is capable of the same opposition with the same results in the world in which he lives.

Jesus Himself attributed disease to Satan, the Prince of darkness: "Ought not this woman, being a daughter of Abraham, whom Satan hath bound, lo, these eighteen years, be loosed from this bond on the Sabbath day?" (Lk. 13:16). "And the seventy returned again with joy, saying, Lord, even the devils are subject unto us through thy name. And he said unto them, I beheld Satan as lightning fall from heaven" (Lk. 10:17-18). We may see a possible reinforcement of this concept of a supernatural origin of disease cited in Jn. 9:1-3: "And as Jesus passed by, he saw a man which was blind from his birth. And his disciples asked him, saying, Master, who did sin, this man, or his parents, that he was born blind? Jesus answered, Neither did this man sin, nor his parents: but that the works of God should be made manifest in him."

While it is clear that much of man's suffering arises as the result of individual and communal sin, there seems to be Biblical evidence for the belief in a universe disordered by supernatural demonic agencies. St. Paul writes: "For our

G

wrestling is not against flesh and blood, but against the principalities, against the powers, against the world-rulers of this darkness, against the spiritual hosts of wickedness in the heavenly places" (Eph. 6:12); and again, "For we know that the whole creation groaneth and travaileth in pain together until now" (Rom. 8:22). We have here a theological doctrine which is too complex to be fully discussed in this place, and we have to acknowledge that if this doctrine of a pre-cosmic fall be true, we have only pushed the difficulty one stage further back.

A passage in *Atonement and the Eucharist*, by William Kerr-Smith (Wells Gardner, Darton & Co., 1901), suggests an answer to this problem of disease in relation to the will of God:

> We ought never to have out of mind that Christ came into the world and took our nature upon Him quite as much with a view to relieve men from pain and other ills incidental to our present estate as from fear of future punishment. We say "incidental" to our present state, because it ought to be clearly perceived that all the circumstances of our lot, even death and hell, which result from sin, are of this character. They are the natural and inevitable sequences of the punishment which the nature of God compelled Him to inflict on sin, but they are not the punishment itself. The punishment was expatriation from the home of God, banishment from the realm of light into the realm of darkness; but the evils which follow in the wake of such expatriation, though, of course, foreknown of God, need not be necessarily, and, in fact, should not be regarded as of His direct inflicting.

Our Lord taught us to pray, "Thy kingdom come; Thy will be done; in earth, as it is in heaven." Clearly this prayer would be meaningless if God's will were not opposed here in earth, so that the implication is that not all that happens here is God's will. Are we not, then, often wrongly attributing many things to God?

In the study of man's physical, mental and spiritual life and environment we are all the time slowly gaining a better understanding of the laws by which God governs us. Our increasing understanding of the physical processes and laws of the Universe extend man's powers. But how often we see the fruits of this knowledge being perverted! As man is permitted to gain power by knowledge, he has a choice set before him: to use it for closer co-operation with God for the good of humanity, or to employ it to his own destruction. Without knowledge of God he cannot do the former, yet God does not will his destruction.

"Thy will be done", then, comes to mean that all advancement in human knowledge and power must be recognised as increasing man's responsibility towards God, for the fear of the Lord is the beginning of wisdom. When man seeks to fulfil God's will and purpose it leads him to all those benefits that God would have him enjoy. "Seek ye first the kingdom of God and his righteousness; and all these things shall be added unto you." All the endeavours of man to overcome disease, to improve his own lot, to advance morally and spiritually, are the indication of a divine impulse within him, but there always remains the temptation to use his growing power to destroy. It is in this conflict that all the pain and sorrows of the world are involved, for the way of life is the way of the Cross. Our Lord's struggle in the Garden of Gethsemane epitomises this conflict, and it is not until it is won by the last awesome act of obedience that He can cry, "It is finished." We see here the great cosmic drama in which we are all engaged and in which we must take our choice on the side of good or evil.

Until we can see our smaller problems against this background of a disordered world in which Christ is the Way, the Truth, and the Life, we shall be dismayed by them. We may think of God's blue-print design for man as that he should be whole, that he should come to the stature of the perfect man, and that in him should be no disease. But to be rid of a sickness is not to be made whole. Salvation can be gained though the body perish; sanctity can increase though the body languish; Jesus has said that it is better to forfeit some physical power rather than lose one's soul. So, though we may rightly believe that disease is contrary to God's intention and that its conquest is in accordance with His will, it is, nevertheless, dangerous to conclude from that that the healing of physical ills is of primary importance.

Prayer and sacrament must be directed first to saving a soul. When physical healing follows, let us be thankful and not at all surprised. Let us by all means range ourselves on God's side as He is on ours, and fight disease and every other evil with all the weapons He provides. But let us not lose faith when we cannot solve all mysteries.

16

THE PROBLEM OF SUFFERING

Who going through the vale of misery use it for a well.
PS. 84:6.

THE foregoing chapters have been an attempt to treat briefly and in outline the leading principles and means of helping the sick through the Church's Ministry of Healing. Wonderful things happen when we apply these principles and use these means. But we are still left with instances of continuing sickness and prolonged suffering. These cannot be ignored, and we must have some help to give to those who are in this condition. Prayer and sacraments are able to uphold and strengthen them, even when healing seems to be delayed or denied. Continued suffering brings its trial of faith to many, and they need all the help that Christian belief can bring to them.

First, we should recognise that we are in the presence of a mystery to which we can bring no adequate answer in terms of human philosophy. Many books have been written on the subject, and in some of them we shall find valuable help for our thinking upon this deep and difficult problem. It is necessary that we should study it, but the kind of argument which we find by way of philosophical study seldom helps when we come face to face with actual instances. The sick-room is no place for cunning arguments. E. Stanley Jones wrote in his book, *Christ and Human Suffering*:

Jesus accepts the fact of human suffering. He does not explain it, much less does He explain it away. Had He undertaken to explain it, His Gospel would have become a philosophy—in which case it would not have been a Gospel. A philosophy undertakes to explain everything and then leaves it as it was. Jesus undertook to explain little, but changed everything in sight. He did not bring a philosophy, but a fact. The fact was His own method of meeting pain and injustice and transforming them into something higher. Out of this fact we gather up our philosophy. First the fact and then the philosophy about the fact—that is the order. The good news is not mere good views. It is the fact of sin and suffering being met and overcome and a way of life blazed out through them—this is the fact of the Gospel.

It would be difficult to put the matter more precisely than that. The Church ministers the Gospel, and the Gospel alone can bring us the way by which victory is to be gained through the dark valley of suffering. The man who suffers without God suffers cruelly; those who walk with Our Lord have the rod and the staff which keep them safe. The suffering which has to be endured can be turned to creative power in the life of the sufferer, and, to quote Stanley Jones again, "Christianity is the only religion that throws nothing away—including frustration and pain and suffering." So the help we can give will not be by justifying the presence of suffering by argument, nor by stoically accepting it as inevitable, and certainly not by either rebellion or bitter resignation, but by sharing it with Christ so that it can become profitable.

Many people succeed in finding their way nearer to God and His heaven in suffering than they could have done in health. But it *is* the way of the Cross, and we who are not called to walk in that way can only pray for those who do, and help them in such ways as we are taught from time to time by the Holy Spirit. Our share is that of Simon the Cyrenian.

This problem of suffering presents a special difficulty to

some who are exponents of the Gospel of healing. They find it hard to accept suffering into their concept of a God Who wills that men should be whole. Nevertheless, the Son of God was not exempted from it. Much of the suffering in the world is the entail of sin, as we saw in Chapter 15. Men who could not suffer would be men who could not feel, could not enjoy, could not strive and achieve things of lasting worth. Nor is the suffering all lost and futile. Some of the finest qualities of human character arise from it.

The Cross represents the full conflict of Christ with the accumulated forces of evil. Jesus did not suffer from disease, it is true, but in His agony—which means struggle—He met the author of all suffering, and the battle was with every form of evil which involved pain of body, mental pain, and spiritual dereliction. It matters not that Jesus did not suffer disease, for He "Himself took our infirmities and bare our sicknesses" (Mt. 8:17).

It has been said that the idea that we should offer to God a diseased body is repulsive, and so it is. But to offer the suffering incident upon sickness is not the same as offering the diseased body. What could be more repulsive than the whole hideous business of crucifixion? Jesus did not offer that. He offered Himself, and to do that He had to offer suffering. There are times when we may do the same. Not to offer it is to withhold a part of our experience, an experience in which Christ shared, and in the withholding we shall suffer defeat. There is a way of the Cross for those who suffer the cruel onslaught of prolonged sickness; but when that suffering is united to Our Lord's there is a way to final triumph. It is the way of tears and bitterness, of bloodshedding and dereliction, but it ends in the final victory of a spirit which is undefeated and redeemed. "Fear not them which kill the body, but are not able to kill the soul: but rather fear him which is able to destroy both soul and body in hell" (Mt. 10:28). Those who can offer their suffering to Christ will not be separated from Him nor utterly defeated.

Two quotations from Juliana of Norwich come to mind: "And he (the Fiend) hath as much sorrow when God giveth him leave to work, as when he worketh not; and that is for that he may never do as ill as he would; for his might is all taken into God's hand." And:

> He said not:
> "Thou shalt not be tempested;
> Thou shalt not be travailed;
> Thou shalt not be afflicted."
> But He said: "Thou shalt not be overcome."

So we do not try to ignore the mystery of suffering nor to explain it away, but to help everyone in his or her day of testing to find that union with Christ which shares all with Him as He with us, knowing that this way there is no defeat. The promise is as true in this setting as in any other connection: "He that endureth to the end shall be saved" (Mt. 10:22*b*).

17

HEALING SERVICES

Great multitudes came together to hear, and to be
healed by him of their infirmities.

LK. 5:15.

THE question of public healing services as distinct from
private ministrations unfortunately introduces a note
of controversy, for opinions differ about the subject
considerably. The report of the Archbishops' Commission
has comment and advice on this matter. It is necessary to
consider the arguments for and against the holding of public
healing services.

Some words from Dr. Maltby's book, *The Significance of
Jesus*, may well be borne in mind:

He gave men healing and He could surely have given them
nothing so unexceptional. But in a very little while, His message
and His mission were in danger of being drowned in the only
kind of miracle they cared about. Frantic crowds were fighting
to get near Him in order to be healed. They would drive Him to
the dilemma either to heal no one or to do nothing but heal. They
left Him but a mere knife-edge to walk upon, but He found the
way, and the principle underlying all His action is the principle
of that choice in the wilderness: men were to be won not bought,
not even with bread, not even with health.

It is true, of course, that Our Lord accepted all who came
to Him and, except that sometimes He tested their faith, he

imposed no selective religious tests. The religious Jew and the Gentile "outsider", even the separatist Samaritan, too, had access to Him and were not denied His mercy and love. On this same principle there are many sincere people who believe that public healing services are justified. It is plain that those who hold this belief have a strong case. There are many, they would say, who will find their way to Christ through their need of physical help and who would not come to Him unless He were freely accessible through the public healing service.

But it is, nevertheless, the considered opinion, arising from experience, of many who formerly supported open public healing services, that there are dangers attendant upon them which are hard to be avoided. What are these dangers?

First, it has to be recognised that there are many "healers" whose teaching and methods are based upon principles and theories which are only superficially Christian and sometimes inconsistent with a full Christian faith. It could even be said that there are occasionally charlatans who are concerned with material profit and others who are pursuing purely sectarian interests. The disillusionment that is liable to result from this confusion is often very damaging both to physical and spiritual well-being. "Healing" is in danger of becoming a fashionable vogue and an end in itself. Signs and wonders are sought for their own sake, and cults which are scarcely distinguishable from pagan magic lead men and women away from God. In days when we have evidence that large numbers of people resort to fortune-tellers, horoscopes, and other pagan types of soothsaying, there is always the danger that the desire to be healed of some physical or mental sickness will be exploited. The confusion in the minds of the public is seen in the popular newspaper articles on "Faith-healing" and in those occasional interviews with "faith-healers" sponsored by television.

Secondly, the mass treatment given in public healing services can and does result in temporary effects which mask the true nature of the sickness and so lead to the neglect of proper medical attention which would often save both life and suffering. Although crowds came to Our Lord to be healed, there is no evidence that He treated them in the manner of these mass-healing services. He took them one by one, and each individual received the attention appropriate to his or her particular need. This is not possible on the scale of an "audience" which could fill the Albert Hall.

Even in the small gatherings at public healing services many neurotics become *habitués* who tend to be confirmed in their neurosis rather than cured of it, and the *malade imaginaire* presents himself or herself to be "cured" of an assortment of ailments which have no real existence, while the basic mental sickness remains untouched. Functional conditions arising from hysteria may find temporary relief, but the cause is seldom if ever eradicated.

For these reasons the public healing service is so often found to be unsatisfactory that, unless adequate safeguards can be provided, it is better to abandon it.

Healing services under the aegis of the parish priest are less subject to this criticism. Where the numbers are few and consist in persons known to the priest, and where proper teaching and individual help can be given, the healing service at the parochial level may be valuable. The necessary follow-up can be made, and the ministrations can be given under a measure of control not possible in the type of public healing service mentioned earlier.

In some parishes Holy Unction and the Laying on of Hands are given at a celebration of the Holy Eucharist. The sick are prepared beforehand and supported by the prayers of the whole congregation. This seems to be ideal, and our churches might well be arranged to accommodate wheeled chairs and couches in a space in the front of the nave. It was my joy on one occasion to minister to a man who had been bedridden for five years with no prospect of improvement. Very soon he was brought to church in a wheeled chair to receive Holy Communion and the Laying on of Hands, and in a comparatively short time he regained a greater measure of health and mobility than anyone had ever expected. He became a regular attender at church, and soon was walking on two sticks to a special seat provided for him close to the Communion rail, and in the course of time he assisted ably in the spring-cleaning of the church and in weeding the paths of the churchyard. His days of confinement to bed were ended, and an electrically controlled wheeled chair enabled him to make happy journeys about the countryside, meeting friends and testifying to God's goodness towards him. Owing to past operations which had limited the use of his legs his healing was partial, but was sufficient for him to enter upon a new and useful life. There must be many who could receive such benefits.

The Guild of St. Raphael exists primarily to secure the restoration of the healing ministry as a normal part of the pastoral care of the parish priest and his people in every parish. This way of bringing the healing power of Christ to His people is, thank God, steadily extending and bearing fruit. Whatever may be the merits or demerits of public healing services, this unostentatious service to the sick is bringing new hope and healing to thousands, and the words of the late Archbishop Lang in an address to the Guild on the occasion of its twenty-first anniversary in 1936 are being proved in many parishes today.

I am sure [the Archbishop said] it is by the quiet and faithful use of the Teaching and Sacraments of the Church that this great power of Spiritual Healing is best realised and exercised. And I believe that this Guild—and I wish it could be said of all similar organisations—is content to work upon these lines. It may be less showy, less spectacular, less sensational than others, but I am satisfied it is working upon the surest lines, and likely to produce the truest results.

18

MIRACLES AND DIVINE HEALING

Every good gift and every perfect boon is from above,
coming down from the Father of lights, with whom
can be no variation, neither shadow that is cast by
turning.

JAS. I :17.

As we have seen, all healing is divine in the sense that
it comes from God, whether by way of the doctor or
of the Church's ministry or of both in combination.
Healing is not less divine when the operation of natural laws
can be traced, and God works through the skills and the
knowledge of physical, mental, and spiritual means which
He has committed to men. God is in control whether the
processes by which He operates are understood by us or lie
beyond the limits of our present knowledge.

This does not exclude the possibility of God's direct intervention in a manner which may be described as miraculous,
but such action is rare if we use the word 'miracle' in its
strict sense. That it does occur is beyond doubt and there are
cases of miracle which have been well attested. Nevertheless,
it is a mistake to think that the Church's ministry of healing
rests only upon such infrequent happenings.

Many enthusiastic supporters of spiritual healing are misled
into claiming miraculous healing without sufficient evidence,
and it is necessary to point out the dangers of making statements and claims of this kind. Popular books on spiritual
healing abound in them, and great harm is done to the cause

by the publication of sensational reports which cannot bear expert examination. Ignorance of some simple medical facts is liable to lead to wrong conclusions, and the sober and invaluable work of the everyday ministry to the sick is opened to suspicion and discredit when the ill-informed make extravagant claims.

The Christian faith rests upon certain events which are styled supernatural. The Incarnation, the Resurrection and the Ascension of Our Lord are direct acts of God breaking through the known natural order. No Christian can deny either these or the miracles of Christ as recorded in the Gospels. By these we are committed to belief in miracles, but we are not required to accept every miracle that purports to have happened in later times. There have, no doubt, been many genuine ones and many spurious. But that miracles can and do occur we must by the premises of our faith admit. Nevertheless, miracles must by the nature of things be infrequent, for God did not create the world to be constantly interfering with the laws by which He has ordained that it shall normally be governed.

The commonest pitfall is to assume that because one event follows another they are causally connected. For example, if a person makes a marvellous recovery after receiving a sacrament, it may be wrongly assumed that the sacrament was the *sole* cause of his restoration. Other factors such as the effect of an operation, or the careful nursing he has received, must be taken into account. Even without the sacrament he might have been cured. This is not to say that the spiritual ministrations were of no value or importance. The mistake arises from ignorance of the character of a miracle.

Certain diseases have characteristic phases during which a remission may occur. The patient is then for a period apparently so much better that complete recovery appears likely. But that period passed, the disease pursues its normal course often to a fatal conclusion. If a period of remission coincides with some spiritual ministration or follows upon intercessory prayer on behalf of the sufferer, it is easy to attribute the "recovery" to that cause. The subsequent decline of the patient is liable to be given no publicity. It is obvious that, when this happens, grave harm may be done to religion.

Again, there is the problem of the "spontaneous cure". Doctors are familiar with instances in which a disease classified as incurable—for example, cancer—suddenly disappears. The explanation of this phenomenon is still awaited. But it should be noted that such occurrences are not always connected with religious ministrations, and that if such a cure follows the Laying on of Hands or Holy Unction or prayer, it cannot be proved that it would not have taken place apart from them. Therefore, no satisfactory conclusion can be reached.

These may be hard facts for supporters of spiritual healing to face, but they cannot be ignored. They serve to illustrate the difficulty of assessing the value of many remarkable healings which are sometimes claimed as being to the credit of spiritual healing alone.

The *Bureau de Constatations* at Lourdes is the only place at which a systematic attempt is made to verify claims of miraculous healing. The fullest possible medical records must be furnished, and a panel of expert doctors examines both them and the patient. Functional ailments and psychological illnesses are not considered, only the cures of organic conditions. If the cure is not explicable by any known natural means and is thus attributed to supernatural intervention, a period appropriate to the particular illness must elapse before a further examination can allow it to be declared permanent. *The Mystery of Lourdes* by Ruth Cranston gives an exhaustive description of the procedure, and should be read by all who are interested in this aspect of supernatural healing. But no such means of investigation is available in this country, and without it it will always be difficult to determine what may be attributed to divine intervention in such a manner as to justify the term 'miracle'.

The value of spiritual healing does not depend upon the occasional miracle which may well occur. Every day through prayer and sacraments sick people are being brought nearer to a healing which they might not receive without it, but most of what is happening is unsensational. The turn of the tide in an illness is often coincident with spiritual help in such a manner as to leave no doubt as to divine assistance; personality changes brought about by surrender to God also change the course of many sicknesses; in many cases the results are of such a marvellous nature that no impartial observer could doubt the efficacy of the unobtrusive and quiet work done by intercessors and by the ordinary parish priest in the course of his normal pastoral care of the sick. Using the word 'miracle' in its wider and freer sense, we may truly declare that there are wonderful works of God occurring every day.

But the purpose of the Church's ministry to the sick is not to establish an impressive record of miraculous events, but to bring God's redeeming power in Christ to bear upon all manner of sickness and disease, and to accept with praise and thanksgiving whatever He deems best for each individual.

Jesus said, "Except ye see signs and wonders, ye will not believe," and again, when the scribes and Pharisees said, "Master, we would see a sign from thee," he answered, "An evil and adulterous generation seeketh after a sign; and there shall no sign be given to it, but the sign of the prophet Jonas." So, too, one of the temptations in the wilderness was to perform a spectacular feat which would convince men that He could do wonders, and the answer was, "Thou shalt not tempt the Lord thy God." Miracles are not granted to satisfy

H

our desire to see a wonder, but to serve a spiritual end. The hand of God is clearly seen by those who know Him, but Herod who "hoped to have seen some miracle done by him", did not have his curiosity satisfied. Jesus was not to be treated as a conjuror doing a "turn".

"Jesus . . . worked miracles because men must see that God is Master in His own world, that our limitations are not His bounds, nor even ultimately *our* bounds" wrote Dr. Maltby (*The Significance of Jesus*). "If they were not received as an outward and visible sign of a Spiritual Presence and an infinite kindness, they were not blessings, but bribes. They did not show God; they hid Him."

There seems to be no reason to deny that Our Lord employed both miraculous and non-miraculous methods of healing. So varied were the means He used that it seems likely that some of His healing works may have fallen into one category and some into the other. Since He was the supreme master of all the means of healing, there appears to be no point in bundling them all into one class. That He had perfect insight where ours is imperfect we should all agree; we grope where He saw clearly, and that is why we are often mystified by His directness and the speed with which He effected His cures. But even if that be true of some of them, there remain many which cannot be accounted for but by the exercise of that divine authority which belonged to Him and commands a miracle. Whether miraculous or otherwise, Christ's healing works were signs of God's love and of the kingdom in which love is the supreme law.

Cardinal Newman in his *Apologia* put forward the theory that at certain times the Church has received what he called "effusions of grace". He believed that these effusions of grace were accompanied by miracles. It may well be that such a period is even now beginning as the Church's faith grows stronger and she seeks more earnestly to be led by the Spirit in meeting the problems of the present age. The growing sense of the sin of disunity and the sincere and humble seeking of God's way of healing it is one indication of a spiritual awakening, and as the Church becomes more ready to respond to the promptings of the Holy Spirit she will become a better and better vehicle of God's grace. Just as miracles have been associated with men and women of outstanding holiness, so may we expect that the Church will recover the miraculous power of healing as she grows in holiness.

As God uses the natural gifts and the knowledge which He has imparted to men to perform many marvellous works, so also the gift of miracle may be entrusted to those whose sanctity makes them suitable instruments to His hand. Only one human being was entrusted to be the vehicle of the greatest of all miracles, the Incarnation, and her complete submission to God's will was expressed when she answered, "Behold the handmaid of the Lord; be it unto me according to thy word."

The gift of miracles is not only mentioned as distinct from the gifts of healing by St. Paul, but is seen in the New Testament to be a gift which is not confined to healing. It is distinct from the gift of healing in two ways. First, a gift of healing may be exercised by the employment of natural processes from which we need not exclude those which are set in train by spiritual ministrations, for, indeed, it is evident that such ministrations often make natural processes more effective, liberating and even accelerating them. But a miracle overrides or changes the course of known natural forces and may reverse their normal consequences. Secondly, the gift of miracle may be used to fulfil some other purpose of God than healing. In the second category come those which are known as nature miracles, but with them we are not directly concerned here.

H*

It may be that the materialistic thought of Western civili-
sation has made the perception of the supernatural more
difficult for us by limiting our concept of what is called
natural, but the supernatural breaks through from time to
time as our faith makes way for it, and, as the saints have
shown us in all ages, the veil between heaven and earth is not
impenetrable. There comes a time when we can say with
Job, "I had heard of thee by the hearing of the ear; but now
mine eye seeth thee" (Job. 42:5).

19

CO-OPERATION BETWEEN CLERGY
AND DOCTORS

For of the most High cometh healing.
ECCLUS. 38:2.

THERE was a time in the early centuries of Christianity when there was no clear separation of the functions of the physician and the priest. Religion and Medicine went hand in hand, and priests and even bishops personally ministered to the sick, treating their ailments and injuries with such remedies as were then available as well as giving them all the spiritual aids the Church afforded. "Houses for Strangers" were provided by small religious communities in which the sick and the aged were given asylum, and many modern hospitals owe their existence to a religious foundation. But as time went on, specialisation in scientific medicine gradually divorced medical practice from its religious connections, and priestly ministrations were confined to the things of the spirit. In the modern Welfare State many other charitable functions formerly discharged by the Church have passed into secular hands. With the growth of population and the many complications in the social order which have grown with it, it was inevitable that this should happen. But it has had the effect of sundering body and soul. This change began at the Renaissance, before which there was no lack of reasoning and logic, but the premises were all Christian. Now a new humanism has taken the place of the old God-centred culture and social order. But perhaps we may see signs of the turning of the wheel full circle as doctors are beginning to realise that man is essentially a spiritual being whose maladies cannot be adequately treated by material means alone. The place of religion in the healing of disease is becoming clearer every day, and groups of doctors and clergy are studying together the various aspects of human ills with which they are jointly concerned.

Reference has frequently been made to a Statement issued by the British Medical Association in a supplement to the *British Medical Journal* in 1947. It has been fully quoted so often that it seems unnecessary to do more than summarise its main points here. They are:

1. The Council of the B.M.A. is of the opinion that there is no ethical reason to prevent medical practitioners from co-operating with the clergy in all cases and more especially those cases in which the doctor in charge of the patient thinks that religious ministrations will conduce to health and peace of mind or will lead to recovery. Such co-operation is often necessary and desirable, and would help to prevent abuses which have arisen through the activities of irresponsible and unqualified persons.

2. Health is more than a physical problem, and the patient's attitude both to illness and to other problems is an important factor in his recovery and adjustment to life. Negative forces such as fear, resentment, jealousy, indulgence, and carelessness play no small part on the level of both personal and national health.

There are certain cults of religious healing, of which Christian Science is best known, which encourage their followers to dispense with medical aid and to rely solely upon faith in God. The results of this doctrine are disastrous both to faith and to the well-being of the sufferer. All knowledge and skill come from God, all material remedies discovered by man to be effective are of His creation. To set them aside is to reject means which God has provided. To rely upon them alone is, of course, to neglect the aid which comes through spiritual realities. The effective treatment of the whole man, body, mind, and spirit, calls for a body-mind-spirit therapy. Each has its place in the Divine economy.

As a scientist a doctor may not be more technically skilled because he is a Christian, but being a Christian he may have his eyes open to many factors in a specific case which are not likely to respond to surgical or laboratory methods alone. These factors are found in the personality of the patient, in his environment both physical and social, and in the depths of his spiritual life. Unless these are attended to, the patient is but a specimen for the laboratory or dissecting room, a cadaver composed of a number of chemical substances. Bio-chemistry may account for physical reactions to drugs, diets, and even for glandular responses to emotional stimuli, but it is necessary to go far beyond these to interpret the complex being called man.

It would be dangerous for the priest to assume the rôle of a psychiatrist without the medical training which it demands, but in the treatment of many maladjustments in the mental life of a sufferer there is an area within which both the psychiatrist and the spiritual physician are involved. Forgiveness for realised sin, and an adequate philosophy of life are ultimately the domain of the specialist in the life of the spirit. The priest must make use of sound psychological knowledge, and it may be thought that the care of souls over the centuries has taught the Church more practical psychology than is contained in many modern text-books. A true religion can bring to a distraught mind a peace and strength which enable a psycho-synthesis to be built up on sure foundations.

The modern investigation into what are known as

psychosomatic ailments is revealing more and more the close relationship between mental states and physical disorders. Where drugs may alleviate symptoms, only the readjustment of the patient's mental attitude towards his daily environment will bring about the removal of the causes of his condition. The stresses of personal relationships in the workshop, the office, or the home, the fears generated by the world situation, and the lack of a sure philosophy of life by which they may be met, are among the factors which give rise to many minor and some major physical diseases. The very term 'psychosomatic' indicates the need of a body-mind treatment in which both the doctor and the minister of religion have their parts to play.

In a broad sense there are no diseases in which the psychosomatic relationship is entirely absent. Disease arouses mental reactions in all of us, and the interplay of the mental upon the physical and the physical upon the mental states of the sufferer is always present. It may show itself in the fear of an operation, or in anxiety for the welfare of dependants; the possibility of the patient's subsequent incapacity, and even ignorance of the true nature of the malady may produce fears which, although sometimes unnecessary, greatly retard recovery.

The general problems of co-operation between clergy and doctors is outside the scope of this book, but it should be understood that such co-operation is highly desirable and that every facility for it should be given by relations and friends of the sick. Doctor and priest together can minister to the whole man, and the most effective treatment makes demands upon them both.

"Honour a physician with the honour due unto him for the uses which ye may have of him: for the Lord hath created him. For of the most High cometh healing. . . . The Lord hath created medicines out of the earth; and he that is wise will not abhor them. . . . With such doth he heal [men], and taketh away their pains. . . . My son, in thy sickness be not negligent: but pray unto the Lord, and he will make thee whole. Leave off from sin, and order thine hands aright, and cleanse thy heart from all wickedness. . . . Then give place to the physician, for the Lord hath created him: let him not go from thee, for thou hast need of him. There is a time when in their hands there is good success. For they shall also pray unto the Lord, that he would prosper that, which they give for ease and remedy to prolong life" (Ecclus. 38:1-14).

20

RESULTS

So shall my word be that goeth forth out of my mouth:
it shall not return unto me void, but it shall accomplish
that which I please, and it shall prosper in the thing
whereto I sent it.

IS. 55:11.

OUGHT we to look for results? Some people would say
"No", but the answer to this question would seem to
be obvious. No human activity is reasonable if it lacks
a purpose and an objective. Divine Healing has as its objective
the bringing to bear upon suffering humanity of the power
which Christ left in the keeping of His Church so that all
may be restored to wholeness. This wholeness, as we have
seen, may suffer enfeeblement in body, mind, or spirit. Thus
the means of healing may be applied to any or all of those
parts of our personality which are affected by disease. In its
fullest sense healing means the restoration of a full and
harmonious relationship between these disorganised elements
of the whole being. We should look, therefore, for the
results of spiritual ministrations as effects which are to be seen
working through the spiritual side of our nature towards
that harmony.

A priest once said to me, "I anointed a man once, but
nothing happened." He was looking for a particular result
and did not see what he expected. But was he right to conclude that nothing happened? When we obey Our Lord's
commands and seek His help in sickness, we can be sure that

some beneficial result will follow. What we cannot do is to decide for ourselves what that result must be. God may have some other and better purpose than that which we have determined upon. Important though bodily health may appear to us, there seem to be times when in God's sight it is not first in importance. "What shall it profit a man, if he shall gain the whole world, and lose his own soul?" asked Jesus. This primarily had reference to a man who had accumulated wealth and come to rely upon it, but it is a question apposite to other conditions. Even bodily health is not the most valuable thing God can give us, nor is it always our most urgent need.

If we lead a sufferer to expect physical healing as the *only* result, we may risk not only the shaking of his faith but his highest good. St. Paul's "thorn in the flesh" remained, but he gained a greater blessing than he prayed for. He realised this more and more as time went on, for in the great strains and sufferings which were to come to him in the course of his work for Christ he learned that "My grace is sufficient for thee: for my strength is made perfect in weakness." Although he was able to bring healing to others, he did not lose faith in God because healing had been denied to him. He came to rely more and more on God and less on his own powers; he discovered that God's purpose is always good, even though it may be achieved in some mysterious ways.

Admittedly, there are times when God's purpose seems to be obscure, when it would look as if our prayers are un-availing to avert the disaster we anticipate. It may even be a matter of some years before we can look back and see how the present good is linked with the seeming ills of the past. But the golden thread of God's wisdom and love is often to be seen running through the vicissitudes of life, and we wonderingly learn that God's ways are not our ways, and that His thoughts are higher than our thoughts. There are times when we must suffer trials of which we cannot see the immediate purpose or the ultimate outcome.

Healing is sometimes delayed. This is especially the case when re-education of the spirit or reintegration of the personality is the only way by which it may come. Much faith and perseverance will then be needed, for there are often obstacles within ourselves which must first be overcome. Wholeness or health in the Christian sense means union with Christ, the dedication of renewed faculties to His service, and the surrender of the will to Him. When the sickness is the outcome of some interior maladjustment or a bad relationship with others, it may well be cured in one form to reappear later in some other. The root cause must be reached, and much of the work of the spiritual healer is concerned with helping the patient to get his life readjusted. The healing of the body, the restoring of the personality, and the reunion of the soul with its Creator, are all parts of Christ's redemptive purpose.

Jesus told His disciples when sending them on their mission to do two things. First, they were to preach the Gospel of the Kingdom, then they were to heal the sick and to say to them, "The kingdom of God is come nigh unto you." Did that not mean that the sovereignty of God was to be a progressive growth in the lives of those relieved, of which the first sign was their restoration? Yet the final purpose of God was not completed whether by the cure of a useless limb or by the dismissal of an evil spirit. Something had been begun, but until the whole life of the individual concerned had become subject to God's rule it could not be said that the work was complete.

So, as God begins His work we may not at once perceive when and where it starts, but when He allows us to see some unmistakable sign let us give praise and thanks for this aid to our faith. If His action has begun in those secret places where it is hidden from our sight, we must not conclude that "nothing happened". "Let us hold fast the confession of our hope that it waver not; for he is faithful that promised" (Heb. 10:23).

Nevertheless, there are many plain and visible results to be seen. My own case-book contains many instances of people snatched from what was expected to be certain death, of health returning after spiritual renewal, and of suffering turned to creative value. Every priest who has ministered to the sick could produce similar instances. Sometimes the "result" has been so quickly evident as to appear to be miraculous. Even in cases where death has brought the ultimate healing, spiritual ministrations have brought cessation of pain, peace, and the joyful acceptance of God's merciful deliverance. The turning-point in many a long illness has plainly been due to the physical reaction which has followed from the spiritual strength gained from the Laying on of Hands or of Holy Unction. The prayers of the faithful have sustained many a sufferer in extreme weakness until the turning-point has been reached.

Nor must we overlook the effect upon some people of being brought to the realisation that sickness is not a curse laid upon them by a wrathful God, but that He is with them and on their side in the combat with the evil that threatens them. This is in itself often enough to bring a new hope and determination to live which turns the scales in favour of recovery. It is very noticeable how a changed concept of God which reveals Him as Love removes the fears and tensions which give rise to much ill-health.

The grace of God works in so many different ways and so naturally that the results frequently appear to be normal enough to attract no special notice. Only those most intimately concerned may discern the operation of the Holy Spirit, while the more distant onlooker sees nothing to cause him to wonder. As a wilting plant that has been re-potted stretches down its roots and begins to live again, so many a languishing invalid returns to normal health when his life is replanted in God. Like the man at the Pool of Bethesda some are waiting for the miracle which they do not really need, for the power is latent within them and waits to be called forth by the word of the Lord. Others like the man with an evil spirit (Mt. 12:43-45) find their lives bedevilled, and the inward conflict destroys even their physical vitality. They gain, perhaps, a temporary relief by a great effort of will, but lapse again and are in consequence less hopeful and more fearful than before. To such as these Spiritual Healing teaches how to fill up the "swept and garnished" room of the soul with faith, hope, and love, with direction and purpose, and with those graces and virtues which turn the negative opposition to evil into the positive acceptance of the Holy Spirit.

The Holy Spirit is as varied in the modes of His operation as are the evils which have to be overcome in the lives of men. As we look for results, then, we must not confine ourselves to a narrow category of physical ailments which we hope to see cured. We must look widely and often far ahead to see how lives are changed, mended, and renewed sometimes with plain physical effects, sometimes with the removal of the clouds which have hung heavily over the mind, and sometimes by the exaltation of the spirit.

The last enemy to be overcome is death. Man cannot for ever be preserved against the separation of body and soul, he can only be prepared for it. From time to time we see a man or woman of great age steadily and quietly slowing down in physical vitality, but retaining a clear mind to the end. The body is wearing out, but the spirit is very much alive. In the presence of these old people we see the gradual approach of a dissolution which, though inevitable, is not accompanied by the ravages of disease. We may feel that this is how God meant the end of man's life here to be. Sometime the body must return to the dust from which it was fashioned, and we shall reverence it to the last moment because it has been the temple of the Holy Ghost. The prolongation of our life here is but to give us more time to serve God, to make ready for that great day when He shall gently call us to Himself. The body, then, is a temporary habitation which, however many times it may be healed of disease, must at last be surrendered. The dissolution of the body and the liberation of the spirit is the ultimate healing, for the soul which has been united to God survives this last penalty of man's sinful state and is at last rescued from the evils which have afflicted both soul and body. In death there is, then, no sting nor victory for the adversary.

But whether we live into a serene old age or whether God calls us sooner, we see in this separation of soul and body the ultimate healing. The Christian hope of eternal life is not just immortality but life with God. Because Christ has opened the Kingdom of Heaven to all believers, the supreme and final result of Christ's redemptive work is seen in the holy death of a Christian.

It should be clear to us, then, that the results of Spiritual Healing are as varied as the ills we seek to remedy, and that because "cure" is not necessarily healing in its fullest sense we must be patient when a cure is not the first manifestation of healing. But it is a daily experience that the grace which this ministry brings to sufferers is leading many back to God and giving them a spiritual strength that is mighty to overcome the ills that afflict them. The results to those who are privileged to see them fully justify our reliance upon Christ's promises to us, and we may well believe that as we continue with faith and perseverance we shall increasingly understand what our Lord meant when He said of His faithful disciple, "Greater works than these shall he do."

BOOKS FOR FURTHER READING

Hubert S. Box, B.D., Ph.D., *Miracles and Critics* (Faith Press)

T. W. Crafer, *The Priest's Vade Mecum* (S.P.C.K.)

Ruth Cranston, *The Mystery of Lourdes* (Evans Brothers)

Evelyn Frost, B.A., B.D., A.K.C., S.Th., Ph.D., *Christian Healing* (Mowbray)

Charles Harris, D.D., Article on 'The Visitation of the Sick' in *Liturgy and Worship* (S.P.C.K.)

A. Graham Ikin, M.A., M.Sc., *The Background of Spiritual Healing* (Allen and Unwin)

—— *New Concepts of Healing, Medical, Psychological and Religious* (Hodder and Stoughton, and the Association Press, New York)

—— *Victory Over Suffering* (Arthur James, Evesham)

E. Stanley Jones, *Christ and Human Suffering* (Hodder and Stoughton)

C. S. Lewis, M.A., D.D., *The Problem of Pain* (Bles)

H. A. Madge, *A Bible Study of Christ's Healing* (The Fellowship Press)

M. M. Martin, *I was Sick and Ye Visited Me* (Faith Press)

A Priest-Doctor, *Christus Integritas* (S.P.C.K.)

The Very Rev. H. C. Robins, *A Guide to Spiritual Healing* (Mowbray)

James Davidson Ross, *Margaret* (Hodder and Stoughton)

R. A. R. Spread, *Stretching Forth Thine Hand to Heal* (Skeffington)

Dr. Paul Tournier, *A Doctor's Casebook in the Light of the Bible* (S.C.M. Press)

Leslie D. Weatherhead, M.A., Ph.D., D.D., *Psychology, Religion and Healing* (Hodder and Stoughton)

The following smaller books are useful for Study Groups and are obtainable from the Guild of St. Raphael, 77 Kinnerton Street, London, S.W.1.

H. Cooper, *Holy Unction: A Practical Guide*

A. H. Purcell Fox, *A Little Book about Holy Unction*

Evelyn Frost, *What is Divine Healing?*
—— *Christianity and Wholeness in the First Three Centuries*
—— *A Talk to Intercessors*
—— *The Healing Church Advances: Our Responsibilities*
—— *A Talk on Christian Healing*
The Church's Ministry of Healing
The Doctor and his Patients—The Priest and His People